skinned

BOOKS BY ANTJIE KROG

POETRY
Dogter van Jefta (Daughter of Jephta) (1970)
Januarie-suite (January Suite) (1972)
Beminde Antarktika (Beloved Antarctica) (1974)
Mannin (Wo-man) (1974)
Otters in bronslaai (Otters in Watercress Salad) (1981)
Jerusalemgangers (Jerusalem-goers) (1985)
Lady Anne (1989)
Gedigte 1989–1995 (Poems) (1995)
Kleur kom nooit alleen nie (Colour Never Comes Alone) (2000)
Down to My Last Skin (2000)
Met woorde soos met kerse (With Words as with Candles) (2002)
Die sterre sê 'tsau' (2004)
The Stars Say 'Tsau' (2004)
Verweerskrif (2006)
Body Bereft (2006)

POETRY FOR CHILDREN
Mankepank en ander monsters (Mankepank and Other
    Monsters) (1989)
Voëls van anderster vere (Birds of Different Feathers) (1992)
Fynbosfeetjies (Fynbos Fairies), with Fiona Moodie (2007)

PROSE
Relaas van 'n moord (Relaying of a Murder) (1995)
Country of My Skull (1998)
A Change of Tongue (2003)
There Was This Goat, with Nosisi Mpolweni and Kopano Ratele
    (2009)
Begging to be Black (2010)

skinned
antjie krog

Seven Stories

NEW YORK

Published in arrangement with Umuzi, an imprint of Random House Struik (Pty) Ltd., Cape Town, South Africa

Seven Stories Press
140 Watts Street
New York, NY 10013
www.sevenstories.com

College professors and middle and high school teachers may order free examination copies of Seven Stories Press titles. To order, visit sevenstories.com/textbook or send a fax on school letterhead to (212) 226-1411.

Book design by Jon Gilbert

Library of Congress Cataloging-in-Publication Data

Krog, Antjie.
  [Poems. Selections. English]
  Skinned / Antjie Krog. -- A Seven Stories Press First edition.
     pages cm
  An original, not previously published, collection of translations
  Translations from Afrikaans and indigenous languages.
  ISBN 978-1-60980-463-3 (hardcover)
  1. Krog, Antjie--Translations into English. I. Title.
  PT6592.21.R6A2 2013
  839.3'615--dc23
                            2013001626

Printed in the United States

9 8 7 6 5 4 3 2 1

CONTENTS

E Body Bereft

9

PUBLISHER'S NOTE

A few things have to be said first when presenting the poems of South African poet Antjie Krog to an American audience: that the poetry in Afrikaans of Antjie Krog was part of South Africa's history for thirty years before the publication of her best known nonfiction work, *Country of My Skull,* a journalist's account of the Truth and Reconciliation Commission that she wrote as a correspondent and which was published here by Random House. At the age of seventeen several of her poems and an essay were awarded a Gold Diploma at the local eisteddfod (a competitive festival of music and literature). These were included in the school's local journal and their explicit political and sexual themes provoked such an angry response from one sector of the rural town's community that the controversy was highlighted in the national Afrikaans Sunday newspaper.

Two of these poems took on a life of their own. Two stanzas in particular of the poem 'My Beautiful Land' caused a political outcry. It reads:

> look, I build myself a land
> where skin colour doesn't count
> only the inner brand of self
>
> where black and white hand in hand
> can bring peace and love
> in my beautiful land

One counterpoint to this melee was the mountain of letters of support sent, mainly by black students, to Krog's school. Several months later an English translation of the poem appeared in the banned ANC mouthpiece in Dar es Salaam. When the first political prisoners were released from Robben Island, Ahmed Kathrada read this poem to an audience of thousands at a mass rally in Soweto at the end of October 1989, mentioning the hope that the words had instilled among those held captive on the island: 'If a school child was saying this, we knew we would be free in our lifetime.'

The other poem, 'Ma,' became a classic among Afrikaans speakers and is, to this day, arguably the most recited, set to music, quoted and taught poem in Afrikaans:

ma

ma I am writing a poem for you
without fancy punctuation
without words that rhyme
without adjectives
just sommer
a barefoot poem—

because you raise me
in your small halting hands
you chisel me with your black eyes
and pointed words
you turn your slate head
you laugh and collapse my tents
but every night you offer me
to your Lord God
your mole-marked ear is my only telephone
your house my only bible
your name my breakwater against life

I am so sorry ma
that I am not
what I so much want to be for you

(translated by Karen Press)

Krog's first volume of poetry, *Daughter of Jephthah*, was published in 1970, two weeks before her eighteenth birthday, and opens with her declaration, in the form of a poem, of what she then regarded as the 'task' of the poet:

daughter of Jephthah

Lord at the Plain of the Vineyards
Lord at Mizpeh in Gilead
Lord God of Jephthah
here is my body!
here is my hymen—safe as a retina
        and whole as a green pomegranate
here is my abdomen—a cold fireplace
        that will watch resigned over the monthly flow
here are my breasts—two bleeding drops
        that will never be leavened with love
here are my hands dear Lord
        strong and willing as my heart
from now on I am Your bride
        impregnated with spirit
from now on I am midwife to a nation
from now on I expect
You

(translated by Karen Press)

Thirteen volumes of poetry by Krog have been published since and she has won virtually all the literary prizes available in Afrikaans and English: the esteemed Hertzog prize, the Dutch/Flemish prize Reina Prinsen Geerligs, the Eugenè Marais prize for best young poet, the RAU prize and Rapport prize for best poetry volumes, as well as the FNB prize for English poetry. Her poetry has been translated into Dutch, French, German, Italian, Spanish, Turkish and Arabic, but not until now has it been published in America.

Dan Simon, New York City, February 2013

Note: Where no translator is named at the the end of a poem, the translator is the poet herself.

AUTHOR'S NOTE

Three themes have fingerprinted my work for four decades: politics and the land, family and love, and the being-ness of the poet. This volume attempts to present a kaleidoscope of how these themes changed and developed in the course of thirteen volumes against the background of profound political and social changes within South Africa.

Skinned opens with poems about writing within the intimacy of family and spans my life from when I met my husband as a fellow classmate at school until our middle-age years, from being lovers, to also being parents and then grandparents.

The second section contains fragments from a volume which is an epic poem based on the life of the highly talented Lady Anne Barnard from Scotland who accompanied her husband to Cape Town and lived in the Cape Castle from 1797 to 1802. I chose Lady Anne as an allegory during the height of apartheid and used the epic form to explore being white, privileged and faced with a landscape that is as utterly beautiful as it is corrupt and unjust. This second part therefore wrestles with a colonial vision.

The third part of this book contains extracts from several speakers who lived in the land before the likes of Lady Anne (and myself) arrived. Through narratives of the First People and inhabitants of the stone desert, glimpses appear of marginalized trajectories. This part also contains a few of the many translations I did from indigenous African languages.

The fourth part represents the political turmoil in South Africa and other parts of Africa as well. The poems come from volumes which examined the often painful, yet also liberating relationships between white and black inhabitants. It concludes with poems about the politics of transformation and belonging as well as the imperatives by which the poet must learn "a change of tongue" in order to be.

The fifth and final section of the book is comprised of poems from a recent book of mine about the dereliction of the body as one ages—the withering body as it navigates meno-pause, a stroke and a lump in the breast.

Some new poems have been selected for translation here from Afrikaans into English that were not previously pub-lished elsewhere, and I have also taken the liberty of chang-ing passages in other poems in small ways from previous translations, as well as shifting content in a few places in order to suit this new collection. It is important to bear in mind that these poems are translations from Afrikaans and are filled with 'writing back' over a period of decades into the rich tradition built by other Afrikaans poets. At the same time, studies of Dutch, English, and German poetry, as well as the translation of literature of South Africa's indigenous languages, have all influenced my work. In this selection you will find specific 'outside' traces of Yehuda Amichai, Hugo Claus, Rita Dove, Carolyn Forché, Rutger Kopland, Gerrit Kouwenaar, Sharon Olds, Dylan Thomas, Gerald Manley Hopkins, William Wordsworth, W B Yeats. The Bushmen narratives adapted into poems can be found in the Bleek and Lloyd Collection, from the Jagger Library at the University of Cape Town.

My sincerest thanks go to Karen Press (*Down to My Last Skin*) and Gus Ferguson (*Body Bereft*) for their impeccable, sensitive and intelligent readings of the first translations. For this final selection I am deeply indebted to Ingrid de Kok, Tony Morphet and Yvette Christiansë for X-ray reading and fearless suggestions.

Antjie Krog, Cape Town, February 2013

poet becoming

to awake one morning into sound
with the antennae of vowel and consonant and diphthong
to calibrate with delicate care the subtlelest
movement of light and loss in sound

to find yourself suddenly kneeling at the audible
palpable outline of a word—searching
for that precise moment in which
a poetic line lights up in sound

when the meaning of a word yields, slips
and then surrenders into tone—from then on
the blood yearns for that infinite pitch of a word
because: the only truth stands skinned in sound

the poet writes poetry with her tongue
yes, she breathes deeply with her ear

(Kleur kom nooit alleen nie, 2000)

marital song

your everyday daily hand in mine
the silence of your thumb
and a palm that is always itself

your hand secretes a mildness
which I fail to name adequately
if you hold me I breathe

our love lords the place
as you weigh in with me until
words convert guile into a glow

of startling light; you can lift me on stilts
and so sterling, dearest, things seldom appear to me
from the edges you pull me back

and convince me to here-ness
to righteousness
for nobody's name's sake

nobody humans language more than you
nobody ignites like you
across borders of leaving and loss

seamless you fathom, fearless you point
out of all you have chosen me but
in the meantime you have turned grey

and awkwardly vulnerable   for myself
you took me in and forged me legitimate
from deep within my lungs I care for you

your integrity fills our length
my eyes open up all around you
I bequeath my mouth to you

you have searched me and known me
you know my downsitting and mine uprising
you understand my heart afar off

but your hand now, this afternoon
thoughtfully in mine, reveals
that we are one flesh   and that

you will die, like me
and like me,
you will do it alone

and not even death, beloved,
can in this
sunder us

(Verweerskrif, 2006)

sonnet of the hot flushes

something staples your marrow somewhere
you feel a newly floated fire spreading angst from
a kernel and how your veins run with fire how
your flesh flames your heart keeps her fireproof
balance your bones bake besides themselves your
face singes your cheeks simmer in dismay and
time and again you break out in sizzling encasings
of sweat you smell your skin sparking off a blaze

but one day you shift in your chair—and
feel this enormous crucible destroying your
last sap   God knows, this is enough:
burning like a warrior you rise—a figurehead of
fire—you grab this death like a runt and plough its nose
right through your fleeced and drybaked cunt

(Verweerskrif, 2006)

writing ode

'Writing is a fraught activity for everyone, of course, male
or female, but women writers seem to have to take stronger
measures, make more peculiar psychic arrangements, than men'
—Janet Malcolm, *The Silent Woman*

to be able to write one has to enter the self
    by going beyond the limits imposed by the self

one has to leave the daylight
the drag of fabricated voices
    and go underground

one travels like a thought

it is quiet there
and completely cut-off
safe   private
one touches down the damp inside
one gropes through the groundless dark
    to find one's voice
to hear the sound of a poem
the line that softly sputters from nowhere

and the writing, the writing down, takes place
    in wrestling the self down

(the man that one loves
waits at ground level
Sundays when late afternoon light slips into stone
he walks against the mountain slopes
the spaces that are not
are not, he says)

this complicates the writing down
and one enters a duel with the self

(the earth groans in the colour of rust
the sun roots brittle blue fires
where then is the word initially safe?
where can it be given an untrammeled birth
before it's tested, tuned and packed for ground level?)

(the vineyard against the slopes
takes a consummate green oath
that nothing will go to pieces
under this tightly stretched wind-blown sky
on moonlit nights you can hear the hoofs
grating stars from the stones
but what do lines like these *say*?
how much colour is sheafed into them?)

I awake somewhere else with a mouth full of lovely words
he, my love
is my heart's rustle and refuge
I want a life simply with him

I do washing in a bath
I am on ground level
I walk out on this morning—brisk of pelvis
    and with steadfast calves
    into the small backyard thrilled with sun
suddenly
    to be dazed by the fragrance of figtree
    sandpaper-leaves and copper

like you, I belong to the earth
and the scars thereof

love flatters in diverse remnants
but there is space for everybody underground
    as middle-aged shadows of each other
until he gets up from the round green chair and says:
I've had enough

and takes down his suitcase
and it becomes dark all around
and one claws up towards light don't
don't let go of us like this
from fall to fall it doesn't matter
but
here it does it does
ever

       one writes: the light licks your face clean
       silver in its tips
       you give yourself away with your eyes

       one writes: this is a morning to die
       against his blameless neck under the eucalyptus
       reeling towards a heretical mouth

       one writes: you eat as if you feast
       I'm frightened by my hunger
          for your planed ankles
       the earth is warm with little frogs

one has everything to lose
one gives up nothing
one balances among wounds, scabs and scar tissue

(the text shudders into its unfettered form underground
one cuts it neatly loose and takes it up
where it plunges one into autumn abruptly
clear
unscathed

leaves sift like coals from the burning trees
like the inconvenient
    and irrefutably too late love of my life)

I *dare* not have underground
I *cannot* live upper ground
from everywhere channels run deep
I search on the wind for a voice to you
my life lies like stone

words do not manage to leave you
words do not manage to keep you
cold bites up from the grass

behind my scarf I say your name your name
and the wind cut snow

never are you out of my thought
you give everything skin
    my life slips away into yours

it had never been difficult
your body is of colour
and nowhere do you hold back from me

I know you more intimately than snare or silk or twine

(how to unlearn you
if only I could hold on tighter)

at times one grows tired of naming
of fighting the angry self down
as underground grief becomes grave for the real ones

⌣

grab me hold my heart
I come not loose from you
I wish you here   your hand turned slightly
forever against the winter fiber of my cheek
entering this ice age—alone
with the thin blue line of mountains in the distance

it's over, I feel you saying
underground from where I am returning
after having lived a futile landscape
not here
here not ever

I no longer function on ground level
I am past all caring
everything breaks loose
what have I lost here?
what do I want here
in this place
where I'm always absent?

it's a morning made for death
I have given up my heart
I live only in my nails

where sleeps my beloved tonight?

⌐

in the meantime it has become winter
you are being pounded into the skeleton of one's heart
supported and suddenly prepared
    one bundles you voetstoots underground
your eyes bleach before memory snaps tight

the heart blows out her last breath
it's the time of endings
never has one loved him so much
as the moment of leaving

but his eyes weather into frames of sadness
his ponytail laced with tuberose slips through one's palm
one misses him
   however many are the days
and the word is grieve

where sleeps my beloved, who calms his rue?
where sleeps my beloved, where sleeps he true?

I walk down foreign streets
my hands deep in my pockets
my body will never forgive me for this

what is left?

god, what does he do on this morning
is he standing forlorn in our white kitchen
hoarse next to the last roses?

⌒

I peel your face
I bite your tongue like a banana from your mouth
burning your language crashes into me

I turn up scorched
the trees are so livid in foreign countries
as your eyes drift towards me in exorbitant light

with you, loveliness and slumber
     are more fundamental than betrayal
the earth rears softly at our feet
in order to belong I went to fetch you

in this geometrical foot of groundlevel space
I touch nothing any more as if it is mine

I want to know where the beloved sleeps tonight?
here or there
groundlevel or lower?
I want to go back to the places where I made us
something in me grew up to find the text
in which anguish turns sound
enduring from then
until now
do not go away
ever from me

(you could have
decided not to desire
to avert
to learn to forget
another skin
you could have)

but when the earth talks to herself
everything desires long-feathered wings

＜＜

after months the underground tunnel
    digs into light
blindly I douse the sun with soft paws
and hear the real one's glad near-sighted laugh: you're here
you're here
ruined we hold on to each other
the earth I cannot bear without you

you sleep, yes
you have come to sleep in me
and your sleep holds everything
you will never sink out of me again
through my word you have stepped into my breath
    with your bony mouth

past our ageing bodies and lost scars
we hold each other
we sink to the ground
we see the face of our dying:

and now one can say it
(in one's fought-for language):
it is *here* where one's beloved sleeps tonight!
and one can call all whom one loves
and say:
listen!
the trees stand drenched with mortality
    everything weeps with transience

I fling our eyes like burning coals into the cold
airily I brush the knuckle of your middlefinger
before us and after us
listen
how the doves drown their sound in the heat
let us breathe carefully past our bruises
death slobbers at our heels

we know that everything will die
all writing and all things written
but this earth
this drizzled breathtaking blue taffeta of earth
not

we touch with newer tenderness

we want to last to watch the earth
and hone language to hold the moment

in this graced word
we belong with each other

touch me
tonight
my decomposing cheek with your fingertip tendril

(Kleur kom nooit alleen nie, 2000)

the men you were

I'm the only one
    who recognizes in you
    all the men you ever were
when I touch you overtaken by tenderness
I touch them all:
the miraculous moon-skin needle-thin elf of my youth
    with luscious overflows of hair
the pooled-in light of your eyes later above our bed
your bony feet in sandals white with knowing and unknowing
    as you hold our first child
my syllables have scuttled many seasons
with you steadying the distances

who has ever fallen so graciously from so many poems?
at times limping but mostly impaled on tenderness
so come, let us celebrate the mercilessness of our discourse
in these times that so pace the light:
this poem is for all the men you are

but I now invite your once effeminate body
to get in here with me in the last stanza—it's fragrant inside
and among the words we can sit in comfortable silences
as the poetry draws blood

the cause of our death would probably be language

(this poem dearest, is nearly what you have thought)

(Gedigte, 1995)

my words of love

my words of love grow more tenuous than the sound of lilac
my language frayed
dazed and softened I feel myself through your stubborn
    struggle

you still hold me close like no-one else
you still choose my side like no-one else
against your chest I lie and I confess
you hunt my every gesture
you catch up with me everywhere
you pull me down between bush and grass
on the footpath you turn me around
so that I must look you in the eye
you kick me in the balls
you shake me by the skin of my neck
you hold me, prick in the back, on the straight and narrow

(Gedigte, 1995)
(translated by Karen Press)

the day surrenders to its sadness

the day surrenders to its sadness
over palm tree and roof the rain reigns mercilessly
the small white house with trellis and high verandah
stands like a warm cow her backside to the rain
eyes tightly shut

inside a woman moves from window to window
as beautiful as sunlight through vine leaves
as beautiful the drops on green
the rain on avocado bark
on the flint stone of leaves
the bougainvillea sparkling wet, sly
keel green on apricots

the double hibiscus groans desperate and red in the dark

the intimacy inside is tangible
children sleeping damp in their room
the man in front of the heater
with art book cigarette and wine   his eyes
glance up somewhat drenched in love

dusk snuffles softly against the gutters
a woman wanders from one steamed window to another
and sees the house constantly from an outside perspective
disabled and thanks to the light in every window
barely conscious of the total magnitude

a warm cow her backside to the rain

(Otters in bronslaai, 1981)

34

illness

the August wind dusts down the street
where I wait for the children in the car
a disconsolate haze hangs over the suburb
low dust fleeces the grass and fluttering daisies
I think of you on a high hospital bed
you have been for so long with me against me of me
I try to imagine you
loose
someone apart from me away from me from us
with difficulty I get you standing apart
loose and with the looseness
a fragility
as you must lie there
slender in your loosely striped pajamas
and I think about how you are being overcome
more and more by this marriage
how surely the weight of it
burdens your thin wrists
how your heart—treacherous from stress—
like a tilting bird swerves behind your ribs

I think of your eyes when you greeted me
how like death they retreated how dry your tongue
how purulent the blister on your lip
what has become of you who are mine—suddenly
the bell and our children
rearing against the wind so pale
so inclined towards each other so frail
so apart as if wind is all they know
you know you are all we have
that holds us together as if related

and I think of you
as of blood I think of you
while we drive on in silence
through this endless dismal August day

(Lady Anne, 1989)

morning tea

while she makes tea something strangely
familiar flows down her inner thigh. like ink.
after many years she bleeds again.

she stands overcome—as if a whole orchard
blossoms up in her throat, as if an old-fashioned
happiness leaks into her body she feels she's

opening shutters towards apples, towards
shades that haze with birds and cicadas
and sweltering distances—as if a

child's laughter overflows in a bath
turning her cheeks vulnerable—intimately
blushed through with daily closeness

as if her abdomen swells young and
strong again around the most beautiful that
she was; her neck gives in to so much light

she carries the tea out onto the stoep
the sky slakes soft for this time of the
morning; the city glistens like a brimming dam

he comes to sit next to her. peacefully he
stirs his tea. in this way they sit
so far left behind in loss and for their age

so carefully rare in closeness

(Verweerskrif, 2006)

how do you say this

I truly don't know how to say this
your seasoned neatly clipped beard is perhaps
too here, too close for language, too grey with grit

I really don't know how to write your ageing body
without using words like 'loss' or 'fatal'. I don't know.
I don't know why the word 'wrinkle' sounds so banal
I simply do not know how ageing should sound in language

in the meantime the irises of your infamous blue eyes
have over the years buckled under green
more stuttering now but two enduring sincere

shadows that have loved me a whole life long
my forefinger traces your eyebrows
from where grey hair crackles like lightning
face that I love; face of erosion

if I pull you towards me your hair is thin and light
your scalp surprises me with its own texture
the grooves cutting down from your ears

the mouth that could scathe so brilliantly still
moves fragrantly against my temples but mild now
—as bread   your hands allow my breasts to sink into
your palms like glasses of dark wine I think I'm

trying to say that I find the thickening of your
abdomen attractive, that an erection against a
slight curve wets the mouth god I think

I'm trying to say that I can surrender to
your thighs for the very first time because of
their soaked-ness, that I prefer the soft
looseness of your buttocks to the young

aggressive passion of our youth you no longer
use sex for yourself but for me you no longer
want to breed children from me but calmly reveal

yourself   into the luxury of experience I
stretch myself   deeper   quieter
as if we come to be much more complete.
at times it seems easier to rage

against the dying of the light
than to eke out
the vocabulary of old age

(Verweerskrif, 2006)

arrivals

1.

at last this lovely little mammoth godawful in roses and blood
straining lovely between my legs tore loose
tumbled, no slipped out besmeared into my arms yelling birth
yelling pain yelling strength oh I throb about this child my
        onlyest my loveliest my smallest my most superlative sound
wash him with colostrum
his arms next to his body wrap him in diapers
in a manger of songs shy murmurs from a twilight room
and feed him
feed him oh feed him free from my heart

(Mannin, 1974)

2.

subdued light bleeds through the half-open door
when you report in glass   breathlight and
heartbreakwhole you surprise us in the night
your first cry plummets my body and my
heart hits the earth. your shoulders stretch and
strain   such a distance you've had to come
to have boer and jew calibrate. how unharmed
you are, how you smell of fresh boracic lint
we bind you in our arms as our tiniest sheaf
of light and peppermint. we host you
in honey, love, from fynbos we dream a tent

but as I hold you my breastbone
rears with pain   then crashes forward
in sparks of flame and firmament

(19 March 2001)

3.

the abundance of her tiny skull we do not
grasp. under her hair, one by one
small leaves fold to bone so that her
little face like a lamp overflows with

light and we can see the rose syllables
of her hands or the rustle of a smile
as it glides up into her newborn eyes
to prevail upon them to stay in this

valley of breath. her feet ladling a glow
as we lay her down in milk and fold
her tight. from so many selves

she's had to salvage her selfest self
before she could arrive as our
tiniest bullet of beloved light

(10 July 2003)

ma will be late

that I come back to you
tired and without memory
that the kitchen door is open I

shuffle in with suitcases hurriedly bought presents
my family's distressed dreams
slink down the corridor the windows stained

with their abandoned language in the hard
bathroom light I brush my teeth
put a pill on my tongue: Thursday

that I walk past where my daughter sleeps
her sheet neatly folded beneath her chin
on the dressing table silkworms rear in gold

that I can pass my sons
frowning like fists against their pillows
their restless undertones bruise the room

that I can rummage a nightie from the drawer
slip into the dark slit behind your back
that the warmth flows across to me

makes me neither poet nor human
in the ambush of breath
I die into woman

(Lady Anne, 1989)

41

transparency of the sole

the light over my desk
streams into darkness
I await my visitors on paper

my four children
finely balanced between anal and dorsal
tiny fins at the throat constantly stirring
eyes uncommonly soft
in the shallow brackish water your mother treads clay
with metaphors

come here across dictionaries and blank pages
how I love this delicate little school
these fish of mine in their four-strong flotilla
lure so close now what should I feed you?

dear child of the lean flank
yield to the seabed
yes the stretching makes you
ache but mother holds you to her mother
is here

the lower eye like father's wondrous blue
migrates cautiously with a complex bunching
of nerve and muscle
till it's up beside the other
pert little mouth almost pulled out of shape
with time the tongue will settle in its groove
pigment of the upper flank beginning to darken

unobtrusive between sand and stone you lie
meshed with bedrock never
again to prey or take flight
I press my mouth against each distended face mother knows

you will survive the tide

(Lady Anne, 1989)
(translated by Denis Hirson)

for my daughter

full of foreboding I sit
sewing name tags
on clothes from which she gleams like sheen through my fingers
her hard shins
and white-gnarled high calcaneus bone
as she walks among other girls

this child holds to me
embraces   shows herself off to me
and I sit   sit sticklike
revolted
and flattered

an unaccustomedness   I want in her
resistance   stand against   turn the back
against the surrender of an enticing body
rather reel from self-confidence my daughter
sharpen your blue dangling eyes
trust the lash of your thick platinum plait

resist my understanding
see my own un-liberation
my inadequate sinewy heart
my entrapment
acknowledge the chill around me
and the absolute fake that I am

on the other hand
do not even bother with this poem from your well-known mother
let it wash down your back
soft   trusting
as you are lying reading on your bed now
you already need no menace
to be so   more
than me

(Gedigte, 1995)

44

for my son

the earth hangs unfinished
and when the wind starts
the child stands in kloof street with his school bag

child of mine! I call to his back
there where my heart is tightest

as always I am elsewhere
I think him into almonds
and arms full of pulled-up light
I trace his whispers in my matrix of blood

shyly the child shoots across the street
the wind takes his orthodontic drool

it is me
your mother
but his eyes are on the brink of leaving me
the earth lies unfinished
the wind splinters from him all that is child
and I tighten about him
past guilt past all neglect

I love him
way
way beyond heart

(Kleur kom nooit alleen nie, 2000)

extenuating circumstances

every word stubbornly tilted into writing
betrays the lunacy
lying just below the vocal cords

all the more strangely it leaks

down the jugular
molars shredding mouth-linings
the breast silts up with something that could be pain

I stretch my hands: for graphite
for paper for language
to come to my sanity
to bring mildness afterwards

in the tidy sitting room on the couch
the youngest skew on his dad's chest
sits my whole family
beheaded
with aortas reeling staining through
    the spittlesoft sounds
    the blubbering blood swabs
I recognise fragments of clothing
and the third child's turned-in fourth toe

under my nails grass splints

(Gedigte, 1995)

man and wife

absent-minded across the table
the lovely wife of an honest man
plays with two grains of rice: round and round
the plate she taps them with her nail

the good man sighs:
she is so pretty!
each day he slips his arm around
her thin white back

he thinks how his nose nuzzles against
her freezing throat: how he melts
the ice in her mouth while his hands
pull the skirt from her legs

but at each meal she sits
absent-minded across the table
pushing two grains of rice
with her nail across the plate

at dark another takes her
he remembers
watching her till midnight
through half-closed lashes, how

her body rocked in lamentation, how
her hands snatched at each other
jumping from the bed, she screamed
but made no sound in the night

then through the streets
the barking dogs, he trailed her, gliding
to the cemetery, and saw her scoop
soil from the nearest grave:

to have the corpse, to scrape
at the rotted flesh with her nails
to gorge that meat like porridge, piece
by piece, to lick the cadaver clean

absent-minded, across the table
the lovely wife of an honest man
plays with two grains of rice, thoughtfully
she taps them   round and round her plate

(Jerusalemgangers, 1985)
(translated by Patrick Cullinan)

as the tale was told

while he undresses
she watches through her lashes
that bloody thick cock
prudish and self-righteous it hangs
head neatly wrinkled and clear cut
about its place between the balls—wincing in her direction

and she thinks of its years and years of conquest
night after fucking night through pregnancies
menstruation   abortion   pill-indifference
sorrow   how many lectures given   honours
received   shopping done with semen dripping
on the everyday pad   from all sides
that blade cuts

that cock goddamit does more than conquer
it determines how generous the mood
how matter-of-fact   how daring the expenditure
standing upright it is bend or open-up
and you better be impress*ed* my sister
not merely lushy or horny
but in bloody awe, yes!
everything every godfucking thing revolves around the
     main*tain*ance of cock

it has no heart no brain no soul
it's dictatorial   a fat-lipped autocrat
it besieges   it's a mister's Mister

she is waiting for the day
in fact is looking forward to the day that cock crumbles
that it doesn't want to
that in a rose-point-pout it swings only hither and dither
that it doesn't ever want to flare
but wiggle-waggles unwillingly
boils over like a jam pot or frrrts away like a balloon

but come it will come
because rumour has it
that for generations
the women in her family *kapater* their men with
yes, with stares
oh jesus, and then slither away like fertile snakes in the grass
taking shit from nobody
and they tell her
her aunts and her nieces and sisters they laugh and tell her
how one's body starts chatting then   how it dances into tune
at last coming home to its own juices

(Gedigte, 1995)

avowal

she sees it coming
the whiskies get darker
the ice less
the jowls begin to hang

then it starts
first a light bitch over trifles
a pretense to rouse aggression
she indulges him and neatly deals with it

then comes the second layer
dark insinuations lugubrious cryptic phrases
she recognizes it and begins the dance in which

every step is payment for betrayal
first she reassures then does penance then
eats dirt, then, at the last chord, shits

(Kleur kom nooit alleen nie, 2000)

paternoster

I stand on a massive rock in the sea at Paternoster
the sea beats strips of light-green foam
    into the air

fearless
I stare down every bloody damn wave
    in the gut as it breaks
the rock quakes under my soles
my upper leg muscles bulge
my pelvis casts out its acquired resigned tilt

like hell! I am rock I am stone I am dune

distinct my tits hiss a copper kettle sound
my hands clasp Moord Bay and Bek Bay
my arms tear ecstatically past my head:
I am
I am
god hears me
a free fucking woman

(Gedigte, 1995)

B

The Lady as Allegory

(from the volume *Lady Anne*, 1989)

Lady Anne Barnard* at the Castle of Good Hope

it is midnight and pewter
outside   from the balcony
the stained gardens breathe
around me   I hear the garrison
and lust after you
already two weeks since you left
at the Imari basin
I imagine you shaving
from behind I burrow into the softer

tack   how robust the seam how virulently
your shirt swells out glides from
ashamed am I of my desire: to grab you by the hips
from behind   grow male
not to ride a broomstick but
to bloody fuck you between tincool buttocks into
        phenomenon

*Lady Anne Barnard (8.12.1750–6.5.1825) was the daughter of James
Lindsay, the Fifth Earl of Balcarres in Scotland. After years of close
friendship with two powerful men, Henry Dundas and William Windham,
she married a commoner, Andrew Barnard, twelve years her junior.
When he was sent as secretary to the Cape of Good Hope in 1797 she
accompanied him and lived in the Castle. She returned to London in 1802,
but Andrew Barnard died before he could join her. Lady Anne left behind
several diaries and countless drawings of life at the early Cape.

'I think I am the first woman'—Lady Anne on Table Mountain

you cannot paint it   colour will fail
the walking into waterfalls ragging
from ravine and stone   around us
the mountain paws the ground and rushes softly
in the mist   everything is held safely
by name
go
please go
why wait   so tiny suddenly
our figures in the gritty trench of words

but your feet beloved mountaineer
in tomato-red socks and climbing boots
move peacefully from stone to stone
to my myopic eyes the mist becomes wiry
our two figures pegged against the rock face
where only damp sweeps between stone and cheek
stained with heather wherever my hands touch
and proteas hang like rucksacks of birds
—colour scrambles ziplike

the climb wipes out
everything between us
we become part of the slippery tongue-talking mountain
my blood pulses thinner than thin
as we go higher and higher
your secure footstep always in front of me
skullwet rain along our hot throats
from Platteklip ridge the wind bores
down on everything which is small and settler

more dense the route—naked
the abyss forces us closer
how do I preserve this memory my fellow poet of beauty
because see: everything is destructible
except the tongue against which we stretch
so small   the soft douche of the sea far below
you turn with the colour of your eyes smudged and lonelier   yes
in your mouth lies the unbearable intimacy of consonance

from above you can really sketch everything
corruption seems only malicious   injustice temporary
and at its worst the village below merely shoddy
see how cute the stonepoint Castle   (my pretty abode!)
oh my God do we have to? yes, we sing: save George our King

the wet clothes in front of the fire
compel us to break through layers of isolation
how do I bring this rainblind trip into words?
hew words for survival
without destroying the breathless costliness
of sheltering each other   both knowing
how mercilessly it destroys this life between   to write

from the Castle at the Cape of Good Hope

they cling transparent ochre to stone and rusted ironwrought
leaves of Capse Rose and Rosa odorata flourish in the fountain
from the Peacock room a strange light devours the inner court

since our arrival this spot has shuddered in my brain
out of autumn gossamer the sun produced a splendid snare
leaves of Capse Rose and Rosa odorata flourish in the fountain

in each draft the light rambles towards you but nought
captures your cape the allure of your neck slightly turned
from the Peacock room a strange light devours the inner court

brittle alabaster your axils where sprigs sprout in textures of tin
threads of woven southern light taken in tow
leaves of Capse Rose and Rosa odorata flourish in the fountain

oh it's only paradise I sought where the sun lords
and drifts towards us in fluent glories of sea and mountain blue
from the Peacock room a strange light devours the inner court

beloved   I have uncovered a continent for us thus bought
by famous apostles to contain all our hesitant ecstasies
leaves of Capse Rose and Rosa odorata flourish in the fountain
from the Peacock room a strange light devours the inner court

Lady Anne Barnard looks out on Table Bay

a new ship arrived.
I prepare parcels and letters
(oh the coming and going of ships
'latest' newspapers, letters
—the written word the only harbour
of the traveling heart)

then the smell hits us—unearthly
so putrid it seems the most primordial
of stenches. it's coming from the bay
says the cook. by midday everybody knows:
a slave ship is unlawfully looking to put to land
609 Congolese—my husband suspects
the hold is under water, a few have drowned; rice, nuts
manioc finished. the obviously greedy upstart
captain of the ship implies that Governor Younge planned it all
while *he* apparently hissed,
'Did you have to hang this maggots' nest
for all and sundry of the Cape to see?'

'But why does it smell so?' 'Annie, in the ship,'
my stolid husband, 'they are lying row upon row—
packed shackled to form filthy strings shelf upon shelf
the doctor does not dare go down because of diarrhea
heat, stench; the deck deadly slippery from mucus and blood.'

I turn the dessert spoon over and over—
silver, expensively heavy and catch myself
for days staring from every window
at the doomed ship in the bay.

at dusk a lament drifts towards the Castle
a kind of howl, sobbing
from the abdomen of that pleading cargo of misery
through my telescope I see on the deck
shackled groups swaying to and fro in a macabre treaty
against death—a shoal of fins circling the ship
waiting for the stiff tussle of bodies
cut loose every morning and thrown overboard.

after I had seen that
'for many days my brain rushed forth
with a dim undetermined sense
of unknown modes of suffering
in my thoughts was a darkness
call it solitude
a blank desertion
no familiar shapes of trees
of sea or sky, no colours of green fields
but huge and mighty forms that do not live
like living men moved slowly through my mind
rotating my soul
penetrating
penetrating walls

Lady Anne looks out again from the Castle of Good Hope

thus begins our new governor:
commission on every slave ship illegally dropping anchor
and the following 'free blacks' executed this morning
for being 'rebellious'

Domingo of Bengale
Moses Aaron of Makassar
Joost Ventura
Sampoernaij Abraham de Vyf
Rebe of Guinee
Jan Coridon
Mira Moor
Kijaija Moeda
and Claas Claasz of Bengale

just a list of heretics
for future composers

they hang this morning
on the open ground
next to the Castle:
a decorative marimba

Lady Anne Barnard: remembered for her parties in my history book

daughter of the House of Lindsay
heroine with the thousand faces
this poem is our final showdown

woman for whom I've sharpened my blade for many years

naked (without possessions) next to your so-called pool
toe nails yellowish   beautiful calves (brutally
I stare) sagging knees   the skin of your thighs

is old apple

your rusty breasts (in paintings
grotesquely bound) has areola and nipple
in one soft point because of no breastfeeding

(despite your drawing of the breastfeeding woman)

your weak abdomen I gather in my hand
it dissolves rennet-like into your fit vagina
gluey this big cream-coloured oyster

how close I am to you my inhibitions set me free

nothing missing in this brief assault
except that you have become beautiful
to me and movingly brave

my head turns to search for your sound in the Castle

my cheek I hold against the dogroses
the steps the water   like a wild shoot
your delicate nose blooms in a showcase downstairs

I bend to touch you overcome with tenderness

your barren hands rattle like reeds
you treated us always like an interesting park
but I look into your thin eyes

sparring blue even here next to your bath

only one life we have
in which we
want to be loved for ever

not opposite but together in this verse

lightfooted and without qualms the water
takes you into its lap I want to hold you
God I've become attached to your

soapy elbows with crayons in clever perspective

your neck stylishly turned somewhat bohemian
in the blonde shavings of your hair
upset I mourn beloved friend

your complete utter radiant uselessness

Lady Anne paints a watercolour of the Mission at Genadendal

before Him
we are all naked
but I see, as always, He sides with them:
the hungry, the poor, the crowds without hope,
the silent stubble, those without rights
He becomes human in this rough building and turns to
      look at me:

it is good that I am here, it is good
I remember my own church—the velvet matrix
with stones and corrupt chattering and I feel
God, how far away from You am I? how narrowly I know
still only myself—tired of white coinage
and they? the brushers of wigs,
the polishers of silver, the whitewashers of walls—
they know apart from themselves also my innermost bed
what do I do? how do I get rid
of this exclusive stain? unexpectedly a song
swells into garish passionate grief
supreme in pain (for the past or what is still to come?)

I sit surrendered in liturgical darkness
my wrists frayed, my lips bleeding densely
my head hangs in the softest sweat
before the closing prayer the missionary folds his hands
relentlessly into the eye of a needle.

I cut the ham into thin fragrant bundles
which the missionaries eat greedily
swiping their forks through mustard
'This you have to taste my brother!'
our Madeira wine runs festively into cups
I don't hear it. I don't see it.
outside the moon grates herself insanely on the mountains

more than millions tonight are huddling close to fires, crude
bread and beer, songs, stories drifting from the coals
how do I give up this snug cavity into which I was born?
Turn! Give! and my overstuffed soul? isn't it simply looking
for something new to thrill about? shouldn't every settler
carry its bundle of gold and rot in regret and guilt—

(even the choice stinks of privilege)

⌒

while the night is still lying in the valley
blood bursts on the peaks. I get up. brushes, inks
water. I drink some coffee, bread, cold meat
my fingers clumsy with my coat. along the footpath
my eyes scout for heights. quickly stretch pages, mix greens,
     yes

green is the colour of balance, green endures
all colours, green is constantly broken
to absorb closer and further
black is only a shade of the deepest green.
in watercolour white is forbidden; dimension
comes from exclusion

I have to find a framework for the complete landscape
if I want to survive, so try: pitch the valley
into perspective, the rest will follow
but something moves between me and the sun
Gaspar the slave holds the umbrella
I wave him impatiently out of the way
but it's too late—
the fixed sun bursts brutally from above
and drums the Mission into mirage

I don't *get* it on paper. it doesn't fit,
the scale is wrong. I aim. I start afresh.
I stare until it dawns on me:
my pages spell 'window', distance
the angle of incidence is always passive
and this is the way Madame lives
here: safely through glass
wrapped in pretty pictures and rhymes
but
I could do: differently . . .
I could slowly pull back my hand and pick up a stone.
        I could throw it
        shatter the glass
        to gasp to thaw (albeit retchingly) in this hip-high
        landscape swirling with wild abundance and abuse

Lady Anne's inland diary

Sunday 14 May 1798
in the lamplight they wait with bunches blond
children, a slave next to every one   the hostess
points to pots of tea and coffee on the coals
'mak-self-knowsbest-vat-like.' dinner:

juicy beef, oryx-stew, stewed
appels, a curry soup of bush partridge on rice
biltong and butter for dessert we are shown
a stinkwood bed with heavy clean bedding

Monday 15 May 1798
early this morning we were in a rocking wagon
over the grassy plains where game stream
until horizons collapse; Egyptian geese
fasten whirring buttons from the grass ostriches

run—their eyes riveted like washers into knobkieries
steenbuck spindly devil's thorn; with fans
flicked open springbuck shoot from the herd-plash;
tails broad as barbells and the glaced lilaback

of plump zebra (I make notes as fast as I can)
with soapy entrances wedged between their hind legs;
among the noise and gunpowder my husband's eyes
gleam with ownership. I both desire and fear

22 May 1798
the one solitary farm house comes to lie
over the next; so also the massive figures
eating: breakfast, fatty lunch
light nap, cake with coffee, fatty dinner

formless women, children shouting at slaves
to their hearts' delight; smelly meat, fleas, dirty sheets
randy daughters watching Mr Barnard's neat morning
ablutions as they polish glasses with a nightcap

Lady Anne leaves the Cape

Andrew follows me with dog eyes. why don't we talk!
I am so aware of my wrinkles, my stained hands
I am really so much older than him—but he seems
to want to say sorry, or, nothing has changed between us
or, I am the best you could get
while you are all that I ever wanted
the ship sent word: I have to board at noon—
loss suddenly has a clear thread

a few Dutch friends wait on the beach
I turn to the mountain: May God protect this land
from sorrow, may it never be destroyed by what freedom demands.
we row to the ship in a flat boat
on the ship I wait at the rails while moving away
from me under salute is: everything, becoming smaller: the marrow
of slavery, tyranny, ignorance, beauty and terror in suspense,
a continent of promise, contours of soul so ultimately generous

it is dark
with small light pools of lanterns
the ship shuffles away into the night.

Lady Anne as guide because a hero needs a bard

I wanted to live a second life through you
Lady Anne Barnard—show it is possible
to hone the truth by pen
to live an honourable life within so much privilege

but from your letters you emerge
hand on the hip talented
but a frivolous fool, pen
in sly ink, snob, naive liberal

being spoilt from your principles
by your useless husband
you never had real pluck
now that your whole puerile life

has arrived on my desk, I go berserk: as metaphor
my Lady, you're not worth a fuck

Lady Anne to Andrew Barnard in the Cape

where will this letter find you best beloved?
if I can choose again
I will not leave you behind there
do not stay away too long

the six walnut seeds curved like tiny brains
did sprout in the cotton wool
I travel everywhere with the small gravure
of your face   at times your eyes look upset

I think about you in the warm Cape
and memories of the mountain the seven feet people
percolate up and how I took all the wrong tubes
of watercolour   oh how I misjudged that brutal
and blissful light   look after yourself

P.S. thank you for the loquat
which left two smooth pips like teeth
in my mouth I miss you
my days are ailing and without you

Andrew Barnard at the Cape to Lady Anne in London

I shudder
when I think
of the distance
between us.
Pray for me
love
as I always do
for you.

I will write
to my Anne
when I get back
from the hinterland.
May the Almighty
keep her
as always.

Lady Anne in Wimpole

the chestnut trees in pots
my hands dirty
when the message came

(but I had a letter yesterday!)
how can it be

how can it be
that that day passed over me
just like any other day?
that I sleep have tea
laugh and potter
while half of me
was already dead?

Lady Anne got back

your slave brought me
a handful of relics:

- a locket with my hair
- a green purse I knitted for you
- your medicine

of fever says Pawell
near Stellenbosch

the doctor from the Cape was too late
there was no-one with you

you are buried on the road to Green Point
a small funeral
and wind from the sea

neither family nor friends says Lady Anne

tonight everything speaks through the dead
    towards me
your brittle bundle of bones
my longestloved beloved
lies lonely and longingly cradled somewhere lost
and lean
I am overwhelmingly awake tonight
of me so little has become
you are all I had in this world
beloved deathling
alone and cold it is behind my ribs
Africa had me giving up all
it is so dark
it is so bleak
soft beloved taunter
of me so little has become
I am down
to my last skin

ending 1

perhaps this ending should belong to me
(so many voices began talking in between)
should the poet survive rather than you Lady Anne?
besotted my hand wades along your neck into cascades of locks
who would ever have known how 'was' we were?
who would have noted your petty flight and entrance who
charted your transformation who showed confounded

what you have participated in? not I says the Bard
I am the great exterminator! from title and trifle
I shall liberate us give us up and shout viva the sole!
(but as ever it depends on why we have come to this continent
the epic heroine's destiny is directly linked to the bard's
can I ever change anything or even bend a border?)
here men live from slogans alone

confused, longingly
I look towards singing into a new ending with you
apart from our miscalculations we have perhaps
been each other's conscious as well
but the most important part of this bankrupt poem
is its farewell to you (hear the gong at the gallows)
and your kind
and your kind's language
from now on you will have to plash elsewhere

under my thumb lies the fine syntax of your throat.

c

Colour Never Comes Alone

nine narratives from the stone-desert in 1999

1. Griet Farmer of Eksteenfontein
'I am very close to cattle
a house is nothing for me
but the open veld
I have length in the open veld
with a round houselet

when we arrived here it was raining
and the daisies were so high that when I
squatted I was sitting under a floor of flowers
from that day I adopted this stony place
and loved it until now
for the disposition
for the veld

2. Maria Johanna Domroch of Kubus
'Grandpapa Mandela for him I voted
why is it that to be a Nama today means something?
why do you come all the way to Kubus?
why am I on television?
because we are now somebody
under the old government we were nothing
over years we have been driven out to the most barren of places
Coloured Reserves
we were nothing
but today we are something
and it is him, that Oldman Mandela, it's him
no, Mandela-them got my vote'

the church in Kubus stands white against the quartzite sky
the ridge blushing with voice
oh God blow and bleed your love on us
says oom Adam
hand on the heart the congregation sings

ja Jissus is the rock
in a thirrr-sty land
in a thirrr-sty land
in a thirrr-sty land
Though art like vapour on me
Jissus Jie-ie-ie-sus

Kubus *hangs* on the ridges of Raisinmountain

3. *old nomadic movement patterns*
"This pattern was completely overturned by the establishment of economic units."
—*Land Use in Namaqualand* by Henry Krohne and Lala Steyn

in the winter the people from Paul's-corner move to Lost-courage,
Hump, Goodmanswater, Ditchling, Dams, One Willow and Pits. the
people from Redfountain pitch their place for grazing at Carpet-thing-
valley, Kammassies, Thickheadkraal and Turn. from Narrowriver lies
the road through Owned-water, Khiribes, Baboonscorner, Hosabes
and Redheight. depending on the rain Spittleriver's people move to
Scissormountain, Wheathigh and Partrichvalley. Stonefountain move to
Newvalley, Greywater and Governmentwell. Two-rivers to Wave-kraal
and Hare-river. Oom Jakobus moves from Ochta to Smallpoxtit and
later to Oena. some years he has to fall back on Ploughmountain, Big-
entrails, Windblow and Kabies.

4. *goatfarmer oom Jakobus de Wet speaks poetry*
'around Jerusalem are mountains
here alone with the goats in the veld
are also mountains
but all around is God
the whole evening I feel Him coming
from this side of Lizard valley

the beginning of me
was at Tattasberg mountain which they now call Richtersveld
herding goats learning how the jackal gorge
    from the buttock to the stomach
the baboon is different

he doesn't catch, he takes he tears open at the hips
    to thread the entrails

my grandchild Benjamin now does the herding
his mouth told this to me this morning
himself he said he wanted to be a goatherd
and I am satisfied
God put into everybody his own talent
at night at the camp the two of us needn't talk
we know where grazing took place and where it should take place
it is a good life to give to a child
every child has his honour
let me say it
it is tasty to be with a grandchild
he makes me laugh
he lets me say untoward things
it is good to be with him

because day and night one is alone here at the post with Christ
we talk
you can lie back
and look at Him with clear eyes
you just have to look
because spirit is always aware of spirit

my goats are earmarked: swallowtail and half moon in front
        try-square and swallowtail on the other ear
government has given me a stud ram
a carcass-holding ram they called it, a real praise goat
among my goats I can never do apartheid
my goats are one
then the blessing of the Lord is there
but if I divide
I will bring my end'

5. the narrative of stone
here! this is stone
only stone
in its stoniest rock-blunt-ugliest stone
trashing all notions of rock, mountain and God
to survive against stone in this stone-desert you need
   God *and* Jesus and a *hell*uva lot of holy soul
or booze
     terrifying amounts of it
because daily it flogs you it fells you down with heat
it scorches you god-black-blind among the stones

look at me! it sizzles
face this brutal weathering these
stone-crunched-flint-flake shards against barren slopes
no cute stone-words to be hacked from here
no chiseling into metaphor no metaphysical fault line
no creepy leave-no-stone-unturned stone talk
oe-oe gall-stone kidney-stone cherrystone
no vomit-inducing lines with grindstone brey-stone
washing-stone stoneware stonewashed stonewall
it shits stone hard here
stone thing here
stone

6. on the banks of the Gariep river
over midday the heat sets firmly in the hills
stones are bleached into blue
at the camp between ebony and karee
Oom Jakobus turns the colon upside down
and spreads kidneyfat like breath over the branches
'bloody shadelet is too shallow' he growls
next to the slaughtered goat

fragile lies the river
open artery in the heat
the stone landscape unthinkable without this scar
older than the oldest human breath on stone

'it feeds my goats of dream and my goats of death'
    says Oom Jakobus
'of nothing too many
of nothing too utterly few'

the mountain on the other side looks as if it's leaking into the blue
the first vygies hiss in cianide
one's watch says: twenty minutes to three
and it means nothing absolutely nothing

I walk behind Benjamin Cloete as he takes his goats to the veld
lightfooted flightfooted he covers the dunes
haii-haii whistles his whip
the goats sink into the overgrown riverbanks
young river reed thorntree raisintree
they munch themselves into silence
Benjamin filters softly into a river willow shade
and now? I ask
'M'am can now catch a slumberling'

7. *narrative of a diamond sorter*
'we empty the gravel bin
and scrape small fans of stone with the gravel knives
and you look and you look
and you see
and your whole body says: diamond!
I am Jan Links from Kommagas
I am 42 years old
I work on the mines from the age of 16
I can work everything: the stripping machine cat 400
cat 769 with the hollow-pedal everything
mine-money is hard money
you remove earth until you get diamond gravel
then yes, then you see now you are here
here is diamond ground and maybe a bit of life ahead
the gravel starts shooting on the conveyor belt
the X-rays pick it up—weight, intensity
and it falls through the flaps into the bins
then we know we know

'here I got to see it for the first time
an alluvial diamond—so rare its shine
its form as if someone has worked on it
even if its brown or green or pink
you feel the shine just blind your body
about the small ones you have doubts
the big ones you just know
here you may never pick up a diamond by hand
you lift it with a tweezer from the water stone and river stone
you put it aside for counting and locking up.
smuggle? maybe at other mines, but not here.'

8. *narrative of another diamond sorter*
'of *course* one smuggles' says Kiewiet Cloete of Kubus
'one smuggles niii-cely
but your nerves they must make it
your nerves must hold fast
because if you steal you have to steal from the sorting table
you cough, you stumble slightly over the gravel on the table
the glue-clay on the side of your hand picks up the diamond
and you and security, everybody watch this thing
but we don't move our heads
we just use the white of our eyecorners
the X-rays scan every second or third man
so you must pick up the rhythm
doves fly illegal ones out to Kubus
or two people tie eland hoofs to their feet
    walking one behind the other to the fence
on the other side four hoofs wait'

9. *the goats*
the goats come home
short woolen waterfalls plunge from the trees
    in the late noon dust
lambs and kraal and goat beards
flickering piss and droppings
whatever they've eaten makes them fart tonight

nothing as soft as kid of goat
nothing as snouty as delicately mouthed
defenselessly eyed as kid of goat
    in the evening when dusk sets in
some get teat   some foreign teat
and its big bleat to flat bleat to smallforlorn bleat
to gay bleat to moan bleat to spoilt bleat
to the vexed bleat of boss bleat

the velvet of a goatling's ear
   slips through the palm
and little horns like horny wings
   which could be pure angel
but the transparent striped eyes of a male goat
speaks of the devil complaining to Satan, says Oom Jakobus

and outside cousin Joseph is preaching
over there on the hill he stands swinging his arms
his voice blown in texts down to us
Joseph preaches for the stones the valleys
to the river he sings
to the goats the night he preaches

but when you begin to see the plenitude, says Maria Johanna
    Domroch from Kubus
that evening
for the first time
the obtuse hills
will ladle light past the tabee tree where you sit

because colour never comes alone here, she says, it never comes alone

(Kleur kom nooit alleen nie, 2000)

/xam narratives (1873–1879)

the wind
(as /Han#kass'o heard in /Xam from his mother)*

the young wind—that is the son of the wind—once was a man
then he became a bird
and he flew, because he could no longer walk as he did earlier
he flew and dwelled in a mountain cave

he who is now flying there, once was a man
once he formed clay and shot an arrow
when he still felt himself to be a man
but then he became a bird
and now dwells in caves
and flies away to look for food
and eats around around and around
and returns and sleeps in the cave

*('/Han#kass'o spoke to me for the first time about the wind,'
writes Lucy Lloyd, 'While he was living with baas Jacob Kotzé.
He told me that the place where he saw this young wind was Haarfontein
/Han#kass'o saw the wind at the mountain of Haarfontein")

I threw a stone to the wind
because I thought it was a *kuerre-kuerre* bird
but then the wind stopped blowing softly
the wind started to churn dust
because I threw a stone at the wind
the wind churned great dust and flew away
it blew hard
it churned dust
the wind burst
the wind that once was a bird

(original recorded by Lucy Lloyd between 1878–1879)

(These three San narratives are based on the texts recorded in /xam and translated by WHI Bleek and Lucy Lloyd in Cape Town by the end of the nineteenth century. It was adapted into poetic versions in my volume The stars say 'tsau', 2004)

what the stars say
/Han#kass'o
(fragment)

the stars take your heart
for they are not a little hungry for you
the stars exchange your heart for a star's heart
the stars take you heart and feed you a star's heart
then you'll never become hungry again

because the stars are saying: 'Tsau! Tsau!'
and the bushmen says the stars curse the eyes of the
    springbok
the stars say: 'Tsau!' they say: 'Tsau! Tsau!'
they curse the eyes of the springbuck

I grow up listening to the stars
the stars saying: 'Tsau! and Tsau!'

it is always summer when they say 'Tsau!'

eaten by a lion

(as told by !Kweiten-ta-//ken)

the lion hunts my grandfather
the lion grabs him and bites him
my father shoots the lion which lies on my grandfather
the lion dies (slowly of poison) as he feasts upon my
    grandfather
my father carries my grandfather home
because the lion has eaten his knees
the lion has chewed up into my grandfather's buttocks
my dad carries my grandfather home
he cuts the tatters off my grandfather's thighs where the
    lion has torn him
my grandfather lies ill, he has been eaten to shreds
his thighs and his buttocks, up into his back
and from that he dies
because the lion has bitten him
because the lion has gorged on his thighs from behind

(original recorded in /xam between 1874–1875)

the young man and the lion

(as told by Diä!kwain, but also by his sister !Kweiten-ta-//ken)

while hunting the young man becomes sleepy
he lies down and falls asleep under a bush
in the heat of the day a lion comes
the lion drags the young man by the neck
the lion drags the man into a blackthorn tree
the lion is thirsty, it leaves to drink water
the lion does not want to be thirsty when it eats a man
the man in the blackthorn tree turns his head
at that moment the lion turns round:
is the man moving? is he still alive?
the lion trots back
the lion moves the man
    so that his head is more comfortable amongst the branches
it licks the tears from the corners of the young man's eyes
the lion licks the tears from the young man's face
the young man looks the lion in the eye
the lion looks the young man steadfastly in the eye licking the tears
the lion trots back to the water

when the lion disappears over the hill
the young man leaps up and runs home
his mother wraps him in hartebees skins
his mother wraps him in mats
she burns herbs so that the lion won't smell him
she covers him with branches

but suddenly then the lion appears on the ridge
the people grab their quivers
they run forward to challenge the lion
they let loose their arrows but nothing happens to the lion
the lion keeps coming

'we have to throw a child to the lion so that it'll leave us alone'
they throw a child in front of the lion
but the lion says: 'I do not want a child
I want the young man whose tears I have licked'

the people throw more children
but the lion ignores them
the people throw assegais
but the lion keeps coming
it claws the huts, it tears them asunder

'we have to throw a girl to the lion so that it leaves us alone'
they throw a girl in front of the lion
but the lion says: 'I do not want a girl
I want the young man whose tears I've licked'
the people stab the lion, but nothing happens
the lion keeps coming
then they call the mother of the young man
'you will have to give your son to the lion
even though he is the child of your heart
or the lion will never leave us, it insists on having your son'

the mother of the young man says:
'I will give my child to the lion
but you will not allow the lion to eat my child
and then let it to walk about
you will kill it when it kills my child
so that it will die when my child dies'

then they take the young man from the hartebeest skins
and give him to the lion
and the lion places his big paws
    on the shoulders of the young man
and bites the young man in his neck
and the people stab the lion, they stab and stab
while the lion bites the young man in his neck

then the lion says: 'now I can die
because I have found the young man I was searching for
I found him'
and the lion dies while lying on the man

the dying young man

(original recorded between 1873–1876)

translations of praise poems from African languages

praise poem for Pheladi

by P Mamogobo

*(translated from Northern Sotho by Matime Nchabeleng, Murray Louw,
P S Groenwald, Annekie Joubert and Antjie Krog)*

Whilst roaming the earth, my eyes were wide open; looking,
intensely searching for the woman on whom I could pour out my
soul—with all the emotions that bewilder my heart. Then I became
pleased by Pheladi—it was she who picked up my emotions. When
I saw her, I was overwhelmed by desire; excited as only a grown
man could be. May the time soon come when she will be old
enough to receive this desire!

Pheladi, light skinned girl-child, secret of my heart
Pheladi, daughter of the Basotho, tiny royal bead of my heart
where have I met you? you, that shake me like a conscience
—you, that even move my diaphragm—you that multiply my
    emotions
you take away my heart, you leave me behind—distracted
I renounce my mother and my sister
and do not smell well to my family: Mamologadi of Phogole
where are you, precious child?
where are you—my unobtrusive luminous cream-child
that made me leave my family behind?
you, that have bereft me of my heart and lungs
your beauty holds me tightly
so tightly that it moulds me into exile
your eyes reflect the black-and-white of cattle loins
they instantly eclipse the stars
they surpass the Morningstar that makes the night legible
your skin glows like a lamp from within
it comes from within and returns with your blood
your blood makes you pure

the colour of your skin surpasses the moon washed by the clouds
you stand, suffused with colostrum from the forefathers' cattle
while you were still curled up in the womb of your mother
your body blotted the purest white
your cheeks and eyes outstrip the zebra with its soft, dappled skin kaross
water in the recesses of rocks—how do you drink it
with a nose as delicately pointed as yours?
do you drink it with the upper part of red ambercane mixed with riddles?
the mouth that I love is filled with the tiny doves of the wives of the ancestors.

Pheladi, you steal my heart like one steals a bone
your hand is stretched out—like a hand searching for lengths of sugar cane
you refused the slender shape, you preferred the fuller figure
you have been crafted for me by the forefathers
the inside of a skin does not render me impatient
because the hand of the kaross clings to your hips
the children return to stiffen the joints of their ankles
the hands of infants stretch their sinews
the nails of them that live in wonder
smooth your cheeks until smooth like the smooth child of a king

you lure me, Pheladi, daughter of the ancestors.
you bewitch me to hysteria, you make me swell like curd
you come to me in the night, your call pierces my dreams
it heralds you
the heart spurs on the soul to possess you completely
Pheladi, my heart falls down: hear me
I cry: because of you my heart and my lungs have grown long in my body
I have been whittled away, I have peace of mind
I quench my thirst and state: I believe
you are twins, pure, you have no sediment
you make the cauldron *blaze* in winter
you remind the night about the whiteness of the moon
your tongue is sweet like that of a little girl
you are as drinkable as the milk of freshly milked milk

Pheladi, you are the secret of my heart
pour my soul out of its calabash
give me back to myself
pry open the fountains for it to flow into the heart of a man
love me
open the fountain-fountains of the rivulets of desire
caress me so that I can borrow the heart
the winglet from the master of the tiny doves

I unfold, I caress the purity of the draw-wells of love
I shiver intensely with desire
a desire that sings like lightning splendid within myself
Pheladi, my fair-faced girl—even her hands are beautiful to me
you are the inheritance
the secret
the true treasure of my heart.

(from Leduleputswa, *1983, Johannesburg: Educum; Afrikaans translation published in*
Met woorde soos met kerse, *2002)*

until you give me a drink of water

by C T Msimang
(translated from the Zulu by P R van Dyk and Antjie Krog)

I shall rise with the Morningstar
and stir up a love potion
I will mix in wild asparagus and palm wine
until you say yes to me
I will go out when the sun slips into its first shine
when the day breaks the first dew
I shall see how you are being led out
by the fragrances of the morning
I will wait for you at the spring
I will wait, I will wait

your spirit I will see
rising with the thick morning mists
    when the hippos come to lie down
my hope will rise likewise
the moment I see you carrying a clay-pot
dark and curved
on your beautifully curved head
the curves of your eyes
yes, light-headed I twirl with all the curves
I bother you, like a bee I stay close to your face
I will keep on bothering you until you allow me to drink of
    your water

I will forever watch over your large kraal
the kraal planted and rooted on the mountain
never will I come greedily
lest I slip down each time
lest my veins bulge, or burst
lest the hill in the end becomes too steep
and you trade me in like expired medicine, destroy my hope

and turn away from me
shun me
become unmoved and mean towards me

no, patiently I will climb the hill
meticulously I will cut the slope
with the calabash violin sing traditional songs
all the songs of expectations
I will skirt the mountain and sing
the mountains bring me near to you
you hear my song in the rough shelter at the gardens where you work
it bangs your chest
it bangs and hammers
until you open and let me in

you who are higher than the trees
even higher than where the birds are
my heart will hang in there
my soul will cling
to the branches of the trees
I will stand unshakeable
empowered by palm wine and burning desire
by the boldness from ardent longings
I beg you, I beg you
let me drink from your water

you who are below all depths
I will descend and strain my path open
like the roots of the wild fig
like the roots of the willow I will go down deep
I will mine like a miner for gold
like a miner for diamonds
even when I thrust onto rock
even when my muscle-power blunts
I will beckon you, I will beckon
until at last you stretch out your hand to me

whether it is red hot or ice cold
nothing will keep me away from you, nothing
the frost covering the mountains
has no power to cover you
even snow or ice
even when the heavens rattle with hail
even if the sky storms down in stormy winds
it will only blow me closer to you
so that you can grab my hand
and give me peace

you who are across the oceans
where the whirlpool rages outrageously like a horned viper
and the waves lash with lashing fury
I will ventilate my heart
I will spread it to become a raft
I will cross the Jordan
and the Red Sea
on my heart I will drift to the Land of Honey and Milk
where I will bring about everything
I will reign with you

you who are above the clouds
my soul bursts with blooms
my soul grows wings like an eagle
swiftly I wing across the universe
I cut waves through the wind
and like Elijah of old
I ride a chariot of fire
I hammer and bang at the gates of heaven
until you who are my life
open up and allow me to taste your fullness

(from Iziziba zo Thukela, *1980, Cape Town: Via Afrika; Afrikaans translation published in* Met woorde soos met kerse, *2002)*

living the moons of the Pedi calendar
(*reworked from* The Pedi *by HO Mönnug, 1967*)

the new year begins with the Initiation-moon in *May*
the Moon-of-harvesting-wheat, yes the Dogstar appears
and abundance can be seen in the beard around its mouth
in May the Divider-of-autumn-and-winter-moon comes
the Full-udder-moon, the Last-sweetcorn-cob-moon

June lets the Last-harvest-moon be
the Master-of-knowing-how-cold-the-wind-cuts-the-back-of-the-
    little-cattle-herder
the Prudent-moon that stashes away

July is time for the Moon-tries-to-cut-through-defeat
    —the first green can be imagined, the Sevenstar hangs
it is the time of the Take-the-last-from-the-trees-moon

in *August* we see the Night-which-consoles-the-chest-moon
it continues into September with its Searcher-for-seed-moon
trees bud in the Reigning-the-backbone-of-the-sowers-moon

October gives the Phato—the Moon-bursting-moon
the Moon-which-let-the-trees-snap-open-with-green
oh then it's time for the Mother-in-law-moon, everybody works

the Falling-moon of *November* allows the impala ewes to birth
    softly into the grass
the dung beetle carries dung into the Insect-without-feeler-moon

December carries its Fountains-flow-in-ample-paths-moon
so that kudu calves graze themselves shining-stomach-round on
    the banks
until Destroyer-moon breaks branches with rain and storms

but finally it is time for the Come-put-it-down-moon
sowing time is over—*January* brings green corn
you sit back and see how the Soft-shuddering-moon
    let grasses and crops shake sifting stomachs of wealth in
      the wind
Sacrifice-moon calls for pumpkin, watermelon and the
      lovely blood of ox

the Worm-moon wriggles in *February*
the I-have-been-warmly-filled-moon
the I-have-done-my-fill-moon

the Trees-bursting-with-seedpods-moon rises in *March*
this is the White-breasted-moon
when ripe cobs hang like the breasts of white women

then it is *April*
April is the First-harvest-moon
the Stern-forcing-you-to-hoe-the-land-moon
but April more and more swells with a terrible moon
the moon of Thinking-all-is-well-but-without-noticing-
      you-have-already-been-gutted
the We-are-the-last-living-by-the-moons-moon
the We-are-the-last-moon

(Afrikaans translation published in Met woorde soos met kerse, *2002)*

praise poem for Desmond and Leah Tutu
on his eightieth birthday

*(Written in Afrikaans by Antjie Krog, translated into Xhosa and translated back
from the Xhosa into Afrikaans by Koos Oosthuysen; final English by Antjie Krog)*

Ahelele! Ahelele!
Sharpen your ears:
Burning beads are gathering at the bottle neck . . .
Words jostle to get out of the mouth. Listen here:

It is I, the daughter of Matjama and Mamtuake, who is singing the praises.
It is I who have come to honour you—I who am of the blood of those of
    the plains.
We have seen how 'my people' behaved,
how they're like pheasants that do not scratch for others.
It is this blood who has come to honour those who redefined the words
    'my people'.
From the red grass and thorn trees I have come to honour and praise you.

I praise today two people who fold into each other like two hands.
The one fits the other like blue buck from the same woods.
The other hand holds the one.
The one washes the other.
At the same time the one hand does not know what the other does,
yet the one carries the other on the hands.
They seldom differ a hand's breadth.
They give each other a hand.
Without each other their hands are tied.

Yes, the daughter of the plains from the Freestate is here to bring praise:
See, here is the Tutu hand from the Tshezi clan,
a hand that is not afraid to be alone in front of thousands of people;
a hand that is not afraid to turn suddenly like a lioness
  and stare the enemy in the eye until they become green;
a hand that is not afraid to stand like a shield
    while the bullets of lies and the spears of spite hit it.

The hand of this man of God can spread the wings of an eagle
and pick up a crowd of people and put them onto abundant plains,
    put them in the protective bight of a river;
    on the mountains of insight and vision,
    in the care of his God.

Because of the prayers from this hand-of-the-eloquent-one the sun
    stood still
        over the townships and also the moon in the Midlands.
With his prayers he weaves the backbone of this country.
He binds us in sheafs and he stacks us—
    the hand of this one-who-is-the-length-of-a-kierie
    [Mdengentonga]
   stacks us into big and mighty roofs;
    he stacks us into shelters for when the sun scorches the hoopoe bird;
    he stacks us into huts that protect against rain and cold;
    he stacks us into structures for the cool gentle breezes of the mornings.

I praise this back that carries the marks of many rejections;
the cheeks that carry the sadness of many humiliations;
the shoulders that carry the scars of someone
    who always says the unheard-of-never-said-before-things;
the shadow that carries the love of a whole country—
a man who spreads great spaces of peace across the world.

Make it known that this hand from this man never makes a fist
    without covering it by another hand.
And it is this mighty palm hand that I will praise now.
Yes, I mean this hand of the woman in the Tutu-household,
    the cover hand, the protective hand.

I praise this hand who is not scared to pull the lion's mane;
the hand who combs the whiskers while scolding,
the hand who easily taps the eagle on the breast,
the hand who spots roads with her eagle eye,
the hand who never hampers prayers,
the hand who kindles fire, peels pumpkin, admonishes, distributes,
who splendidly walks in front knowing the roads,
the hand that distinguishes lightning from the cloud until the truth
    radiates;
the perennial hand,
the directive hand.

When this hand takes the other hand by the hand
Then this couple forms an indestructible handgrip.

I can continue praising,
But like the star with the tail I disappear,
ndee gram!

Table Mountain rondeau in four parts

'Table Mountain symbolized all that is strange and enigmatic to an "outsider" looking in at the Cape of Good Hope.'
Hoerikwaggo—Images of Table Mountain, Nicolaas Vergunst

Table Mountain and Table Bay were called Hoerikwaggo (Sea Mountain) and Camissa (Place of Sweet Waters) by the Khoi. Later arrivals alternatively named it Cabo da Boa Esperança (Cape of Good Hope), Golfo Dentro das Serras (Gulf within Mountains), Cape of Storms, Mons Mensa, Montagne de la Table, Tafelbergh, d'Klipman, Table Hill and Table Rock. In Zulu myth it was referred to as Umlindi Wemingizimu (Watcher of the South). It was also the Portal to Africa, Guardian of the City, the Old Grey Father of colonialism and the Silent Witness of apartheid.

1.
from inside   from outside
from in outside   from out inside
from innermost outside to outermost inside
from inner and outer namegivers to inner and outermost mountain

from inside Camissa from inside sweet water
from inside Camissa from outside fresh water
from innermost inside fresh water fresh sweet
from inside from outside

from outside Golfo   from outside Golfo Dentro
from outside Golfo Dentro das Serras from outside
from outside Golfo
from outside from inside

from inner outside from outer outside
from masterful namegivers to mountain from sea
from outermost inside to innermost outside

I see a foyer   I see a guardian
I see a place   I see only sweet water
from inside from outside
from naming from taking
from refuge from subterfuge
from mountain from sea   from mountain as table
from inside from outside
from innermost inside from outermost inside

from hope   from apart
from apostle   from governor
from chief of taking   from chief of giving
from trade place from storm place
from god place from give place
from taking and taking
from taking

2.
from inside   from outside
from in outside   from out inside
from innermost outside to outermost inside
from inner and outer namegivers to inner and outermost mountain

from inside Camissa from inside sweet water
from inside Camissa from outside fresh water
from innermost inside fresh water fresh sweet
from inside from outside

from outside Golfo   from outside Golfo Dentro
from outside Golfo Dentro das Serras from outside
from outside Golfo
from outside from inside

from inside out from outside out
from masterful namegivers to mountain from sea
from outermost inside to innermost outside

from Table Mountain Klipman   from outside Mons Mensa
from inside from outside
from inside out from outside in
from table of stone from inside from outside
Mons Mensa of stone and from outside
Mons Mensa of stone and from Mensa
Hoerikwaggo from inside from outside
from innermost outside Hoerikwaggo from outside
Hoerikwaggo from inside Hoerikwaggo from outside
Hoerikwaggo from innermost outside

without religion from outside
they are animals from inside
animals without souls from inside
from outside

without souls from inside
they're doomed from outside
have no rights from inside
acknowledged from outside

on land   on life
on living stock   on after life

3.
from inside   from outside
from in outside   from out inside
from innermost outside to outermost inside
from inner and outer namegivers to inner and outermost mountain

from inside Camissa from inside sweet water
from inside Camissa from outside fresh water
from innermost inside fresh water fresh sweet
from inside from outside

from outside Golfo   from outside Golfo Dentro
from outside Golfo Dentro das Serras from outside
from outside Golfo
from outside from inside

from inside out from outside out
from masterful namegivers to mountain from sea
from outermost inside to innermost outside

Umlindi
Umlindi We
Umlindi Wemingizi
Umlindi Wemingizimu
from inside from outside
from innermost outside Umlindi
Umlindi Wemingizimu
Umlindi kwaggo
Hoeri Umlindi
Hoerikwaggo Umlindi
Umlindi Wemingizimu Hoerikwaggo Mons Mensa

mountains from outside are the world from inside
and outside is inside and inside now outside

some ascend mountains to see far
some ascend mountains to lay down the self
some ascend mountains to flee
some simply live on the slopes

some ascend mountains to test themselves
some ascend mountains to create borders
some ascend mountains to honour
some live in caves
simply on slopes

some ascend mountains to rule from there
some ascend mountains to chisel the gods
from in-less outside from out-less outside
outermost out-less outside
outermost out-less from outside

some live lightly on slopes
some only adore
some watch
how inside and outside are going to pieces

4.
from inside   from outside
from in outside   from out inside
from innermost outside to outermost inside
from inner and outer namegivers to inner and outermost mountain

from inside Camissa from inside sweet water
from inside Camissa from outside fresh water
from innermost inside fresh water fresh sweet
from inside from outside

from outside Golfo   from outside Golfo Dentro
from outside Golfo Dentro das Serras from outside
from outside Golfo
from outside from inside

inside out blows outside out
from outermost inside blows innermost outside
from outside blows inside
in-outside blow-inside
out-innermost out   blows outermost in
from blow-innerside outmost
from outblowerside inmost
from blust from blin
from blustblin minsside
blusside
blssd
blessed

(Verweerskrif, 2006)

D

Vernacular White

land

under orders from my ancestors you were occupied
had I language I could write for you were land my land

but me you never wanted
no matter how I stretched to lie down
in rustling blue gums
in cattle lowering horns into Diepvlei
rippling the quivering jowls drink
in silky tassels in dripping gum
in thorn trees that have slid down into emptiness

me you never wanted
me you could never endure
time and again you shook me off
you rolled me out
land, slowly I became nameless in my mouth

now you are fought over
negotiated divided paddocked sold stolen mortgaged
I want to go underground with you land
land that would not have me
land that never belonged to me

land that I love more fruitlessly than before

(Gedigte, 1994)
(translated by Karen Press)

Bessie*

the quilt—blue smocked with foam—
is finished off in golden facings of sand
spreading softly to all sides
lusikisiki lusikisiki
the reeds say from the seams
wood from the wreck is cut from the blue
on the beach lies a washed-up child
I am Bessie I am Bessie
she cries against the rocks

they carry her to the village
they name her Gquma: Tongue-of-the-Bellowing-Sea
they mark the white calves for her
they bring the washed up brushes
for the lukewarm honey hair   the hair only of her
say the Mpondo

when the last wooden partition gives up
china drifts from the perished crates . . .
spreads
slowly over the ocean floor
perfect little cups tilt   a vase slips
bubbling loose from its lid
blue-and-white saucers wobble in the soft sand
for a soundless tea party—
the voices of the drowned wade out on the waves
Bessie Bessie they cry against the rocks

after decades whites journeyed with outstretched
hands: Bessie, we're rescuing you
come with us to the Cape

the wife of Tshomane refuses.   since
then, from history, she has been haplographied

(Jerusalemgangers, 1985)

*Bessie was a seven-year-old European castaway found on a beach in the
Eastern Cape in the late 1600s*

every day I treat you as if you were mine

after an eighteenth-century engraving of Table Mountain*

We know that when one crosses the equator everything becomes
Wilderness: white becomes black, good becomes bad, culture becomes
A kind of barbarism in which nothing has a name:
Women throw a tit over the shoulder
Cannibals, winged lions, vulvas hanging down to the knees
One-eyed people bark and snakes stand upright in the trees.

Nobody will ever believe our relief when, one morning, we saw this
Table—something simply so miraculously ordinary in the wilderness
—something so civilised one at last could pin a memory there.
That's why, when we named it, we didn't honour any
God or king, but simply threw a big party on the
Southern tip and baptised it 'Table Mountain'.

Now, listen carefully: because I had named you, I let you
Rise somewhat higher in my engraving—up—like a real
Table. So that with you as backdrop we could throw our arms
Northward, we could stylize your skyline against the wilderness
And, as famous logo, send you home, yes—we learnt
Quickly how the crumbs fall from international tables.

I draw your tabletop neatly—nothing will hang skew.
To the side of the bay I put those who we say call themselves Hottentots.
They eat raw intestines and look! to have his cow give milk, this man
blows into her bloody c . . . t. One has to know one's bearings here,
      or what am
I talking about? To turn you into legend against the wilderness
I pull you slightly more to the front—that's it, your feet close to shore.

Windeberg and Leeukop, a formal request—please throw your arms open
As if to embrace. To me it looks, and forgive me if I overestimate
Your reaching out, as if you and this continent have groaneth and
Travaileth in pain until you could be delivered into glorious liberty

By the children of God. Every piece of property I number and name
As they rise stepwise against your slopes—say what you want

But we did bring so much order to this place that on my engraving
I can add cultivated gardens blooming in the wilderness. And while
I'm at it, let me show the church somewhat larger in scale. Next to
    the jetty
There, let's have the gallows—you never know, you know—this bay
Hangs full of heavily laden ships anchoring at this Place of Name.
For colour I plant two flags flying over order against the chaos.

(Whatever this engraving adds, whatever it leaves out, however wide
One casts the eye or carefully names—the mountain was the
    forerunner
Of how apartheid and forgiveness were applied against a
    continent's clamour)

(Verweerskrif, 2006)

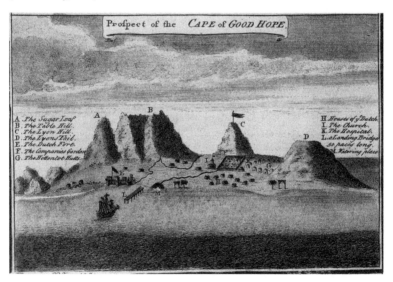

* *'Prospect of the Cape of Good Hope' Plate 199. No114. Vol. 2 p.404. Collection of the
Iziko Museum.*

scar-

by which name do we summon dreams
other than the obsolete name God?
that which simultaneously liberate and oppress
what is it in the word white?

what gives it a better sound than black?
say it: both lie equally on the tongue
from which meat do whites grow so high?
oh the guts not to be windbag or jackal

but mighty tree blooming into the all-self
suffering should   liberate
us all into seasons of consciousness

forefather, our blackening blood demands:
a redistribution of pain

-tissue

the scar of the eyes
is the wound of the body
a harmed-through body

in primary suture the edges fit exactly:
a clean wound can heal
to a thin-clean scar-line

in secondary suture the tissue is injured
the skin has to grow from the edges like kikuyu
but skin does not grow horizontally
and skin comes only once on the palm or foot
that is why scars always come with colour

scars are most rarely in bone:
there where we resemble others the most
there we decompose slowest

(Jerusalemgangers, 1985 & Kleur kom nooi alleen nie, 2000)

lament

death trots through the dark
without sound
without rustle
a sudden clip of metal
and death trotting along the footpath
trotting
trotting
wrist-flexing, furrowing death
(there's yesterday and tomorrow but
    it's now
that's unbearable)
in footsole and cartilage death trots forth
      trots through the dark

on a blade-blinded night in April
the long held-back scream screamed

out of fear, out of insanity, out of foaming anguish
the hacked ones fell in embraces of blood
note the mother with her child hacked to her pelvis
note the pink panty notched into a femur
note the set of teeth hacked vertically
note the prickly pear mash under the mortar

note how every limb blindly averts
how every face is turned away
how every arm tries to invent her own silence

only death alone knows
that the hand of a brother
rules deadlier than the deadliest god-head gridlock

without sound without rustle
death trots on in the dark
trotting
trotting
hacking, furrowing, flexing, disemboweling death
      trotting forth in the footpath
(there's yesterday
and tomorrow but it's the
scream
that's impossible)
in the darkglitter heart of Rwanda
the longheld blacknight scream screamed

note how the hills awake in sediments of blood
note the unseemly spectacle of bones
      rising in the plantations
note the bodies rafting down the banks
crows, coffee, avocado trees, honey, dogs,
fish—a complete firmament fed from blood

death trots forth in boots my boots
three hundred and thirty deaths per hour
without sound it arrives
without rustle
death trotting through the dark
dour, bedraggled, dogged death
trot-trotting trotting
(there's yesterday's tomorrow, today has no name)
(today has no space it plumbs it plumbs . . .
it plumbs the abysses of slave of plunder of colonize of race
        of rape of apartness)

note how lip and tongue and eye and heart
have never endured
but note how the skeletons are no longer obvious
        as man or woman
        white or black
the skeletons are inescapably
        indivertibly
        humanlessly human
slaughtered by the hands of the already dead

killing—killing a bereft body has burst its heart
the black glittering cold heart of us all

(Kigali/Butare, June 2000, first published in Kleur kom nooit alleen nie, *2000)*

letter-poem lullaby for Ntombizana Atoo

1.
hush-hush
hush-a-bye sweet
sleep soft
sleep whole
born wet   born now

outside orbits the earth
so ah and you
so bloused in blue

let wind take your nostrils
let earth take eyes take ears and tongue
let fire let rain take your skin

hush-hush
hush-a-bye sweet
sleep soft
sleep whole

2.
the wind is all over the sky
with my voice on its way to you
you who lie irrefutably stippled
somewhere in cloth and herb
in songlets and pain
your vertebrae curving against what's to come

oh that you could see the earth
clinging with suns and moons and comets and meteorites
the wind-filtered sky
in tufts of fire tomatoes fly out among leaves
the moon reports in milk
in the thorn trees next to the road

the stars hum their way to you
you have to see
you have to hear how the sun lures the wind over your threshold
taste how the water changes to still ivory plates in the setting sun

childling, the earth glows of heaven

3.
I will come and claim you from bones and bullets and violence and aids
from muteness from stupidity from the corrupt faces of men
I'll gather you from millions of refugees
from hunger and thirst from the damp of cries and the stink of
     tolerated grief
the desperate mangle of dreams
from the back I'll recognise the brave stalk of your neck
I will catch up with you
and pull you out by the arm

because you have to see differently
for us of the abyss
we all have to balance differently
this continent drifting like a big black plundered heart on the globe
continent that is us
continent throbbing in its vast ventricles of desert and forest
continent on which so many figures commit deeds of forlorn trust
big aggressive heart on which hundreds die daily without sound
decaying in heaps
into raking brooms of bones

I want it to be you my smallest
that between your ribs
you have to feel the tremor that things have to be different
that something has to become true of what we are

that what we are is something so soft so humanly skinned
so profoundly constitutionally big and light and kind as soul
so caring as to surpass all understanding

we are what we are because we are of each other

why then do we keep on being so wrong?

I lay my cheek next to yours
I want to breathe into us
to care
to care

4.
join your shoulder blades into tiny wings
breast the roaming despair
next to your mother who sleeps with her head turned towards you
do you hear me?
everything is so lucid tonight
your mouth has loosened a little from the breast
do you hear me?
I who am all-that-is-white
who am lightningwhite and indissolubly always only myself
I want to be taught by you
and bask this morose mumbling heart
cradle it so
that it splays out its clogged crooked valves
that it rigs its full sails to the wind and navigates
the earth in celebration

it's dark outside
a chain rustles and I hear magazines slip off into the grass
I stop breathing and bend over you
my finger touching your fist
which slips open and holds me immediately
tightly
your mother stirs

loveliest thinniken thing I have just come to say welcome!
and that something of me will go with you
and that you needn't know of it

child of mine
child of morrow
with wild plaits and cheeky slender neck
it is you, one day, making poems along the dusty road
    who will sing forward the way . . .

  yes! I see you

(Kleur kom nooit alleen nie, 2000)

toilet poem

things of course about which one would never write a poem
force their way into the territory of poetic themes
such as changing tampon and pad to pee in toilets
of townships where one comes

on the floor water and effluent almost ankle deep
I wade on adidas soles like a cat

no moveable equipment available
like toilet seats bins hooks locks doors

my jacket hangs around my neck in blanket folds
handbag clutched between teeth

tampon—swollen red mouse, stained pad
wrapped in bank counterfoils

I piss shuddering rigid half squatting
between my legs

into a toilet bowl heaped halfway up
with at least four different colours of shit

every nerve ending erect with revulsion, poised to go mad
if just one drop should splash against me

(Gedigte, 1995)
(translated by Karen Press)

nightmare of A Samuel born Krog

the desk is warm and bloody like a newly slaughtered
    carcass
from the drawers transparent synovial fluid drips
the chair against my back becomes big and pulpy
knocks and croaks like a frog
the clothes on my body take on a life of their own
they rear like snakes and breathe like fish
my tongue jumps around tail upright acrimonious
the salivary glands rattle their pincers
my hand falls on the white breath of the page
an animal with fur on its back
the pen becomes a soft hairy nicotine-stained finger
the letters it writes listlessly start decomposing at once
books swell with indignation
the keyboard grinds its shallow teeth

I write because I am outraged

(Otters in bronslaai, 1981)

a one dimensional song for the northern Freestate, more specifically Middenspruit*

most beloved state of heart estranged from spring
where maize crackles like stars
with rust-blond beards distilling the moonlight
where sunflower fields spread handkerchiefs in the valleys
where clouds roll like horses
the late sun shoots out peacock feathers
across plump and broody fluff-green hills
each farm dam windmilled with willows
evening's last sparks fizzling
through heron-still waters

most beloved state of heart estranged from spring
where trains with ferns of smoke
go easily clicking and clucking each winter
over redgrass flecked with sparrow wings
over khakibush and blackjack echoing ironstone and
          guineafowl
reedbrown sandstonebrown dassiebrown winterbrown
white leghorn tufts in marshes
where partridges wobble like vetkoek at twilight
every winter morning cracks apart—sharp as needles
a crisp willow-whip splits the frost
the far-off puff of dung fires
autumn feeding only on poplars
power-lines chattering softly to each other

*Middenspruit is the farm near Kroonstad, Freestate, where I grew up as part
of the fifth generation.

most beloved plains of my heart
where the jack-knife of winter
casts itself completely
into the green harvest of summer
so many years I've tried to deaden our tie
and make your plains fertile in some other way
but each season I come to trace you again and again
for if I die this way I die
with your redgrass month-in month-out
blossoming my eyes

(Otters in bronslaai, 1981)
(translated by Denis Hirson)

in transit—a cycle of the early nineties

(a)
first Christmas weekend under the
state of emergency 1988
we murmur on the verandah at dusk
it's as if ears stir in the ivy
strung in blood around the house and fences
unexpected forms wait in the shade
we hesitate
opened letters fall into the house
someone runs up the street
we wait
the garden rustles in mists of suspicion
we speak more softly
so many children in prison
so many arrests
the trains moan restlessly
is it true
so many thousands of children?
rumours crawl from the foundations like rats

christmas cookies ginger beer a little tree
children play with cousins
the turkey hisses stuffed with tarragon thyme and raisins
under bows of light families bob in boats
the river slushes against the keels
crackers crack
black workers at the mooring place look up
unfathomably

I play the piano my children dressed
as Mary and Joseph and angel sing:
  away in a manger
  a trough for his bed

(translated by Karen Press)

129

(b)

refused march at Kroonstad Monday 23 October 1989
        my thirty-seventh year to heaven
I wake up in my town that I can only
          experience as backward in flat air-conditioned
               little shops jails with rose streamers
                  fluttering fragrance
the house embraced by a scorching wind on this day
the day of my birthday while thousands
               start crowding close
          on the small greened square between town
and township: the march through my town today

        ten I asked for   perhaps we'll find ten
ten whites who want to see the town reconciled the way it
        wants to spread its own freedom over cool
           banks   crickets carve the midday
           bare and willows smell
like bark   for the sake of ten of eight don't be angry
for the sake of five, alright then, of three for the sake
              of three don't destroy
              the town   sulphur and fire
hold back so that we can occupy it over again, new

        roses gasp salmon-tongued from their buds at tea delicate
sandwiches light murmuring of peace
        spoilt gifts heartfelt wishes
              I know the march should now be heading to the left
              as far as the main street
here I sit with everything white—thus I fail completely   my tongue too thin
my writing too stuttering my language uncertain
        of hand and flees
               to paper   purblind town and all that burns
is my fist beside my own salt pillar of fear

(translated by Karen Press)

(c)

Brentpark march 1990
how to write this land
how to say it arm in arm   row upon row
fluttering in front our minister's coat
the steel wall
yellow casspirs
bandoliers with fingerthick bullets
a slit-eyed policemen let the chain slip
the alsatian yaws up to my face as if possessed
cold soots the wind

my heart tolls heavy and dull like a decomposing pear
on the casspir a man from my neighbourhood
his teeth gnarling venom
another kicks open the door of the police van
and curses all kaffirfuckers

slowly the procession
our first march in silence
from the little bridge on the fringe of the coloured area
we have been allowed to march a meagre five metres
a landscape completely stops breathing
we stand up   we stand together
we clasp arms   we hear a strength flowing from us
see:
we march therefore we are

bullets crack   violent assaulting sounds
lightfooted we sow in all directions
hide in unknown backyards slink along fences
get one by one back to the scene of the crime
everybody tells his eyes
we laugh and shudder
we touch one another again and again

a march with a hundred eyes has scorched us a new skin

(d)

1992

stones against the corrugated iron of the school's roof
a window bursts inward

automatically I wipe the splinters from the table
take an empty page   sharpen my pencil
let the shavings fall god knows neatly into a tissue
instinctively I begin writing
another round of shards
children yell   someone's hand is bleeding
another window and another . . .
Darrel runs past me—a dagger in his hand
his eyes glitter as if from somewhere else
the boys in the class pull from their pockets:
penknives, daggers, bottlenecks, screwdrivers
something burns   somebody shrieks rhythmically
against the door frame a pupil is pushed
a knife protruding next to his balls
a blot bleeds on his threadbare pants
a window smashes in my face
I dive down under my table—pencil in hand
I'm starving for a cigarette is jesus the only thought in my head

if a stone hits me I'll die
I will simply   just
die
anyway already suffocating from the violation of space
of property of privacy of life
on ridges where nobody's life has any worth

under the table I try to get hold of the word
a single word enabling me from this side to transgress

132

(e)
1994 (before the election)
decades of death in the valleys
where white families disintegrate—overweight
and bewildered they sit deeper into their houses
bullying thicklegged sons at loggerheads
in front of the tv timorous daughters take to their heels
wives wrinkle moist in frills
while the patriarch coughs on the toilet

behind the broken border fences
chicken pens rust among khakibush and weed
next to crumbling troughs devil thorns lie lush
telephone poles tumble on fallow fields
nobody scans the borders anymore

under the searing heat of the hardboard ceiling
on fake leather sofas their fingers lock around ice cold beer
fuck the kaffirs
has finally changed into
the fucking kaffirs

(f)
1995 (after the election)
I say it beforehand
loud
I stand for nothing
I join ranks with nowhere
nobody comes near me

all of them look the same
all are men all
are necks all
pods of power

the generals and brigadiers and ministers
and headmen-generals sit cuddling their cocks

plaiting their penises
trashing a whole country with the alternating faces
of politics and violence
all are sly
all feel fuckall

Lord from whence cometh our salvation?
in the corridors lie money and glass
stop streets of meat
taxis become gargoyles of blood
and everybody wants to have
and everybody wants to keep
between nobody nothing nowhere gets healed
between nowhere and nobody nothing survives
nobody offers
nothing
          vapour
nothing
          balming
nothing   something
          healing
something gentle
something mildly human

I say it beforehand
I stand for nothing
I join ranks with no-one

I repugn completely

litany

here along the long white shadow
where I thought where I thought I'd leave the litany of locust
of locust and death I'll always hear the litany of sound

here along the long white shadow
where I grab lustre grab honour that once was lustre and white
the truth I've heard and how to molest it

that I travel I travel along the corn or chaff of my past
that my past crawls forth on its deadly knees without once looking up
that I claw on my knees claw to that place

that light place that does not want to dim
here along the long white shadow of mortal and molested truth
we buried many we buried without shroud or ritual

many we buried and from the graves it sprouts
the shadow sprouts of lustre, burdock and wheat the locusts of sound
here along the long white shadow

and my past sits so well in its teeth all along
its teeth sit well in the shadow of sulphur and lime it's time
the time of assassin and shame and tin

I keep slipping slipping out of truth
while next to me along the long white shadow walks the shudder
that I was walks the long white shudder of ash

set me I who keep slipping in the long white shadow
out of time out of random and lies I want slipping from the shudder
along the emptiness of litany and shadow

set me set me from revenge and loss
from ruin set me from the long white scar the lichen and ash set me
free into remorse oh my hand my hand grabs the sheet like a throat

(written in 1996 during the first Truth and Reconciliation hearings and published in
Country of my Skull, *1998)*

some seasonal observations of Table Mountain

WINTER
friday 8 may
fog falls like
a fainting spell
and wisps float free from black
umbrella pines. the mountain
has no form
no figure, no measure to
surrender   rain
chills
down its stony back. at noon
the gun fires. sound muffles
double
then fades into fog—
threads of fog
fog plunges soundlessly from
the cliffs

thursday 14 June
this morning the mountain withdraws
itself from speech. it refuses to
broach itself. its chest of
stone is still concealed with copious
steaming wings like when it
rained on and on for a thousand years
—toothless it grumbles in the fog, yet
when it does lift its kaross for
an instant: sinew-white a
newborn waterfall flashes to light

tuesday 27 June
is it the severing from the other
continent
forty million years back

that makes you
endure unyieldingly over
the bay? that was the day,
they say, that all the stone in you
cracked. that part, as you know,
never returns to one.

SUMMER
saturday 18 december
like a big
flickering butterfly of stone
the mountain quivers

in the heat.
the city bowl shrieks like a hot
cauldron. its breath breaks

into flames.
searing, the cicadas singe the
peripheries black.

behind a
gas flame the mountain rages with
heat, with fire, with a

scorching blaze
of hatred. are you perhaps in
a basket of shade,

or in the
purple silver breath of a wild
olive? is the

light sweat on
your upper lip a sacrifice
to allow you to

kneel down with
both knees planted?

sunday 22 january
fog already steals across the bay.
Blouberg's point bleeds into the
sky. it looks as if a white powder puff
is shaken out, as
if rhinoceros grass evinces a

haze, as if the mountain
groans in the heat. the helicopter
whips up a thimble of
water from the reservoir, and fades
into smoke round Devil's
Peak—just to swerve jauntily over

the bay and cool its sting
in the sea. the city bowl drones. the
air smells of pyres.
with sheer sounds the starlings swoop
from the loquat tree

later the burnt mountain skims its pointed
pivot of silence over
the bay—a dove gives it breath, and
a falcon
spreads its far-flung wingspan

saturday 28 january
your stone remembers when
the earth was still soft to the touch
your stone remembers when the
first creeping beast ascended you
the fynbos remembers when
you were alone, just you and the wind
and the blue white bay; your
shape remembers the exact moment
when a human eye first
beheld you and made you time

sunday 5 february
thousands on your outskirts survive
on a different silhouette
for how many aeons more will you
observe how we don't settle the case?

monday 6 february
steadily the days curve
more brightly blossoms
are crushed by the wind. on
some inclines I shall never walk
again. from the earliest
times you have been identified daily

and appropriated with
eyes and inhalations
that methodically flaked you off.
my heart knows that you have
nothing to do with us, that you are

lost deep in the concept
of mountain, that the word mountain is
an abstract noun, that blue
is a verb, stone a friend, for next to
you I become she and
she he and we   irrevocably

you remain. all incantations of yearning
tilt in my chest. my pulse resounds with
poems and axillary
feathers, my blazing gizzard

buzzes with rhyme. I hone
my heart to yours. words my mouth
will lose—skins will become undone
as we learn
the changes of tongue

thursday 2 february
unyielding the mountain keeps its
stone amassed between distribution
and redistribution,
advantage and previously disad-
vantaged—because the more she's abused for loot

or ideology,
the more she moults and shakes herself clean;
the more the arrogant
die against her cliffs, roads and suburbs and
detours choke up against
her, the stronger the wind she rams down

her kloofs—the decay of
human memory evidently
insignificant on
her face.

friday 3 february
              just when they think she's theirs,
she heaves her mighty head
scornfully erect to the sky and

reveals her body in a
resounding triumph of
mountain. majestic she stands there, clamorous
in a fucking larynx of radiant

ruin—my god, I am
covered in goosebumps. this she will do long
after we'd fallen back from her

—de-heavened

(Verweerskrif, 2004, after ten years of democracy)
(translated by Andries Wessels)

country of grief and grace

(a)
between you and me
how desperately
how it aches
how desperately it aches between you and me

so much hurt for truth
so much destruction
so little left for survival

where do we go from here

your voice slung
in anger
over the solid cold length of our past

how long does it take
for a voice
to reach another

in this country held bleeding between us

(b)
in the beginning is seeing
seeing for ages
filling the head with ash
no air
no tendril
now to seeing speaking is added
and the eye plunges into the wounds of anger
seizing the surge of language by its soft bare skull
hear oh hear
the voices all the voices
all baptised in syllables of blood and belonging
this country belongs to the voices who live in it
it lies at the feet at last

of the stories of saffron and amber
angel hair and barbs
dew and hay and hurt

(c)
speechless I stand
whence will words now come?
for us the doers
the hesitant
we who hang quivering and ill
from this soundless space of an Afrikaner past?
what does one say?
what the hell does one do
with this load of decrowned skeletons origins shame and ash?
the country of my conscience
is disappearing forever like a sheet in the dark

(d)
because of you
this country no longer lies
between us but within

it breathes becalmed
after being wounded
in its wondrous throat

in the cradle of my skull
it sings   it ignites
my tongue   my inner ear   the cavity of heart
shudders towards the outline
new in soft intimate clicks and gutturals

I am changed for ever   I want to say
forgive me
forgive me
forgive me

you whom I have wronged, please
take me

with you

(e)
this body bereft
this blind tortured throat

the price of this country of death
is the size of a heart

grief comes so lonely
as the voices of the anguished drown on the wind

you do not lie down
you open up a pathway with slow sad steps
you cut me loose

into light—lovelier, lighter and braver than song

may I hold you my sister
in this warm fragile unfolding of the word humane

(f)
what does one do with the old
which already robustly stinks with the new
the old virus slyly manning the newly installed valves
how does one recognise the old
        with its racism and slime
its unchanging possessive pronoun
what is the past tense of the word hate
what is the symptom of brutalised blood
of pain that did not want to become language
                could not become language

what does one do with the old
how do you become yourself among others
how do you become whole
how do you get released into understanding
how do you make good
how do you cut clean
how close can the tongue teeters to tenderness
or the cheek to forgiveness

a moment
a line which says: from this point onwards
    it is going to sound differently
because all our words lie next to one another on the table
    now
shivering in the colour of human
we know each other well
each other's scalp and smell   each other's blood
we know the deepest sound of each other's kidneys in the
    night
we are slowly each other
anew
new
and here it starts

(g)
(but if the old is not guilty
does not confess
then of course the new is also not guilty
could not be held accountable
if it repeats the old

things may then continue as before
but in a different shade)

(1998, when the Truth and Reconciliation Commission closed down, published in Kleur kom nooit alleen nie, *2000)*

becomings

A group of African poets was invited in December 1999 by
the Gorée Institute to follow the slave route backwards from
Gorée Island (Senegal) to Timbuktu (Mali), traveling for weeks
by bus, train, pinnace, and performing with local griots at
every stopover. My fellow travelers were: Thierno Seydou Sall
(Senegal), Were Were Liking (Cameroon), Chirikure Chirikure
and Chenjerai Hove (Zimbabwe), Zein al Abdin Fouad (Egypt),
Eraf Hawad (Central Sahara) and Amina Saïd (Tunis).

1. (CITADEL)

you have become my word for native
for nailing me as from-here or not-from-here

it is true! my forefathers carefully recorded
their greed: golden rooftops on the horizon

rivers where gold slimes the banks where
winds open a flaxen footpath at your feet

I look for the truth
of what I am

you will tell me—that much I know
mud-citadel still of the mind

2. (BEGINNING: Gorée)

we start at the door from where no-one
had turned back   the door of slaves
keening is what we find at the threshold

keening, and the imagined footfall of those who
could not choose whose bodies were turned
into one direction and their blood into another

we are here to intercept something of
the lethal equilibrium between the direction
of the body and the direction of the longing

here at the edge of an endless pending
continent and trailing darkening seas
Dakar Kaolack and the stupor of being

disemboweled
                              from others

3. (GRIOT SONGS)

'we are the guardians of memory   we eat
the words we utter   the grain of the word
is the culture of mercy   we are the carpenters
of memory   we shave words'

'there is the dignity of the word
the nobility of the word   the place
of the word in a room   we are
the master-transmitters of the link'

'not only the word but the journey of the word
the footprint of the consonant   the journey towards
that word'   'the griot is the double shadow of mankind'

'to see the word pass in the foyer of language
is to found the place of breath'

4. (GRIOT'S STORY TOLD ON THE NIGER)

'when the sun sets in the cold seasons the light is ochre
as ochre as a ripe citron
the evenings are as ochre as the skin of a Fulani girl
who only drinks milk and eats meat

in the house of the Bambaras
was Bollo Ole
as beautiful and fleeting as the glow of a lance
as enchanting was Bollo Ole
her eyes married the wettest black
with the milkiest white
yes, those were the unforgettable eyes of Bollo Ole
no-one in the country was more beautiful than she
people started quivering when they saw her
some became obsessed
if you put a finger in their eyes
they didn't even blink

Bollo was so beautiful that she did not understand shame
Bollo wore no shawl
no camisole, no gown
Bollo wore nothing over her breasts
Bollo was so beautiful that she had no shame

the whole wood danced
the whole wood swayed
the birds, the animals frisked the early morning
    during the song of the griot
suddenly something stroked the back of the griot's neck
something soft was unfolding in his neck
slowly he turned around and saw a young man
an indescribably beautiful young man

it was Samba Diam Werdi
Diam Werdi loosened his hair and shook his head
so that his hair rushed soundlessly to his hips
this is the man for Bollo Ole
this is the man as beautiful as she

the griot taught Samba Diam Werdi
"this is how you love a woman:
Idji is the left breast
Idji Adia is the right one
Idji Algoukubou is where it is moist between the breasts
Idjy balakti idji
is where the upper-breast fastens onto the chest
    the slight slope of it your nose must know
Idji reiyati is where the breast swells towards the armpit
that your tongue must know
Idji al Mouroufou is the tenderest side of the breast
    below where the plump overflows the palm . . .
about the secrets of the ochre areola we will talk later
but remember:
if a woman pounds seeds
and she doesn't sweat slightly between her breasts
don't marry her"

the Tuaregs were on their way
white their flapping gabeyes
white their billowing gowns
white the turbans and scarves
white the determined harnesses of horses
eye-white white were the horses of the Tuaregs

down rosy dunes
they plunged
in a furious terrifying white for
Samba! A! Samba!

Bollo urgently massaged Samba's breast from his thighs
the slave massaged her master's legs from the feet
Bollo saw
the enormous cloud from the feet of the Tuaregs
she knew they were coming
   for the sleeping Samba Diam Werdi
Samba! A! Samba!

when they left
the beautiful Samba's body
became transparent in the lightning of the blade
that killed him

Samba! Oh! Samba Diam Werdi!'

5. (RIVER: N'ger-n-gereo)

bank of reed
bank of silt
bank of dune and silence and creek
from the shoulders of water
one by one   slip
the soundless scarves of sand

river
river of rivers
Nile of the Negro
Niger
river unlike any other
sunk in memory and the sediment of blood

every flow makes its choice
'but the Niger has many mouths
the Niger destroys the single mouth'
'the Niger promises deep slits of oxygen'
'the Niger melts no borders to its flanks'

in the mist
in the colour of mirror and silence
steel and mercury
eggshell and milk
the sun sets like a moon

a wild glare of water flares at my feet
how not to touch it with language
and yet burn this collar of radiance on the retina
its cool plunge of air
its first stay of star

'flatten yourself over the Niger—
its blessing,' its lustre, its bliss
among flow and lisp   keening
and connection skate soundlessly light
without vowels of memory   oh memory

'when river is beloved
we walk on water'

7. (BEVERAGE)

until the end there was coffee
satchels nescafé-instant-granule-coffee

in fact satchels nescafé-instant-granule-coffee
was the only constant on the journey

milk changed from pasteurized to raw
to goat to tins of instant breast milk

deep, and to hell and gone, no milk no
electricity but, nescafé. nescafé-granule-instant

the emptying of such a satchel on the tongue in
the desert produced, well, a rapture of its own

8. (BOAT)

the pinnace carves the river
the pinnace slices down the thin cincture of land
the pinnace buttons water and sky together
blinding-blue and lime in the sharp midday hour

'the river knows no boundaries'
'the river touches all sides'
the river makes possible more than one form of being

spreadeagled over the ribs of the pinnace
one lies with every fingertip open
something loosens in this lure
not of being
but of becoming

many

many

becomings

9. (FREE FROM THE TYRANNY OF ONE)

dare light slip so soft
dare sand reel so free

dare skin say so much
in this search for an identity?

skin has many colours in Afrika
the heart many shapes

not the colour of skin
but where the heart enmeshes

(look, in the water
it's always there: the omnipresent whiteliness
sitting like this, like this, gesticulating 'truth')

10. (POET BECOMING)

Albacaye, Mountaga and Tidiane kneel against the dune
in the plaincoloured shavings of their robes
when they sit up straight—facing Mecca
each forehead carries a blond blazon of sand

when dusk implodes in our midst
silence feeds down from a freight of stars
poetry comes   coming from a crackling
of languages, accents, memory, translations:

'the woman with the whitest eyes
folds a cloth around her breasts
whether she said 'come in' or 'be greeted'
I do not remember
I was lost
may Allah make her mine
before I lose my mind'

'my horses
the moon
the dunes
they know me'

'when they break my pen
my words take fire
when they destroy my horses and camels
my teeth hang from their wrists
when they squash my breath
I scorch their palms
I am the revolution! I am the nomad!
I live everywhere'

'I don't think, I sing
I am the poet of silence'

'I am the vagabond of the word, the nomad'
'I swindle with the silence of words, because I live in them
they are my tent and my waterhole, my everywhere
    tegument'

'poetry is always busy with light'
'the scars in tongues can write
    landscapes of breath
but it has to glow from the inside'
'it has to smell humane'
it has to 'embrace the shoulders of the stranger'
'poetry is the ritual of draping sound
over the unheard so as to live opened'

I breathe
suddenly I breathe
light-footed and loose-limbed
I breathe from a seam slowly sutured
from scar-tissue colour and skin

(Kleur kom nooit alleen nie, 2000)

E

Body Bereft

it is true

it is true that this landscape will
continue to exist without me the trees
that make me adore the earth the plains
that sweep into seams of light-lipped
water that mirrors the nearest
seams of touch the moon living
off a stipend of new born stars
it is true that it will continue to exist

it is true that I saw three women
naked on the beach at Marseilles their
bodies like three bags of wrinkles their hair
like tissues in the wind. with short steps they
padded into the water their breasts wrinkle-less
forming a halo of flesh of steaming risen
breasts blushing into their nipples it is
true that I couldn't keep my eyes off them

it is true that I saw in a shop window three
kinds of nappies for the aged, bedpans,
fungicide, bedsore ointments and something
that looked like a potato peeler it is true that
as of late I stare intensely at old people how
they put their feet down or wear their hair that I
lay my eyes desperately on young skin and fluent
bodies it is true that I'm on the brink of an abyss

since

since we started walking
this road the irises have
finished blooming the still
abandoned eyeballs of the
light blue ones, the plush
folded bats of the purple

row. since we started this
road the grass has been gasping
away seed, the buttercups have
dropped their leaves like nail
clippings, the camellia's
bathrobe among the cedars

has withered from the
branches since we started
the road. the tough pony-
tails of the wisteria
have fallen into disrepute
the banksia-waterfall

has finished her fatal
plunge since we started
walking this road. the
swallows have come back we
can smell the jasmine from
its jugular, the snow has

melted from the mountains.
since we started a man
tumbled backwards into
the air   what we breathe
is the air of all this
world the sky overwhelmed

as a witness of grief. at
dusk we become dark
of tongue as we translate
disintegration our
ankles reek mortal but
god how strong our thighs have

become since we walked this
road how fierce how savage
our filigree as the
heart bangs its terror

five menopausal sonnets

like death in my arms

you come and sit this morning like death in my arms
I am so tired I can hardly breathe. you say
what has been promised by whom?
what is written in the weathering of our bodies?
our life together walks its own destructive road
I am independent and totally unreliable you say
I am tired of being questioned, of being watched, tested
I say you are fed up being lied to with frantic explanations

and I? I want nothing   I do not want to be anything
to anybody   I do not want to belong anywhere   I want
to fall free—suddenly and colourless like a stone

one thing I'm learning
the more I destroy you the more
I myself am run into the ground

bronze bull of Lavigny

the upright stance is wearing him down
the forever-young torso is getting to him
his over-indulged chest is slipping in between
his legs as he drags the blonde fields uphill in

a remembered act of bliss—his hide skinned
by seasons of poets feeling him up for metaphors
his balls rust forth, his thighs shuffle
protectively around the sweet decomposing

chamber of lust. what is he to do now—this
sad solitary bull? his tail sprained. one horn
gone. his body has become one dumb
eroding dump of fear among the trees. he

knows the great collapse is here and pushes his dry
derelict snout up among the mauve pertblue plums

short visit

the child is leaving. I'm left standing.
well-known eyes meet before the sunglasses.
hands grapple while the safety belt.
the street desolate. I wave, wave. as

all light pales. as everything aspires
bleaker. as the heart refuses.
everything that should have been said.
after every visit I devise.

next time to explain the scorching.
I undertake ways.
I utter what binds us. you want to

hear so little. the unsaid bloodshot desperate
fistblow. whether it had hit the snout.
full out. jesus! I am bleeding, child

hormone sonnet

to hrt
or not to hrt
is a question
only for women

it implies: do you want to look younger,
get cancer and Alzheimer's
or do you want to look old
and live too long?

if I ask my mother about menopause
she looks at me as if I've said the word 'internet'
'didn't you ever get hot flushes?'

'my girl, when I sweated I assumed
it was from work and then I went
swimming or simply took a shower'

God, Death, Love

God, Death, Love, Loneliness, Man
are Important Themes in Literature
menstruation, childbirth, menopause, puberty
marriage are not

meanwhile terror lies exactly in how
one lives with the disintegrating body
in how one accepts that the body no longer
wants to intensify with exhilarating detonations

in how one loves the more-and-more-slaked-ones
in how one resigns to vaginal atrophy and incontinence
or that the blade cleaving through one's heart
is probably a heart attack

to jump from the ageing body to Death
has suddenly become a cop-out act

leave me a lonely began

'the voice of the menopausal woman is feared
and denied. She has been made invisible or
encouraged to remain forever young . . .'
—*Tamara Slayton*

he sits across, reading his newspaper
his coffee waits timorously next
to his precisely clipped nails. his
hairy ear busting with gunpowder. his

shaven cheeks brittle. suddenly he looks
up and shouts to the back: 'coffee shop's
empty, we can close!' and she realises: he
does not see her. she sits as nothing. that where she

is is simply air or glass or emptiness
he did not *not* see her, or perchance look
past—he looked right *through* her. she's
vanished without tamper or trauma;

to the waiter she's merely table-leg or chair
how did it come to this where nothing
exists any longer that acknowledge her
as a woman? nothing that recognises

that she carries the cool shape of a human
who loves the earth and this late coffee
on the square where soft seeds waft
the midday air? her silent invisibility

bends her eyes to her hand playing
with crumbs on the blue check table
cloth. and it is so: every finger joint
is thickened and stiffening into a

new direction. next to the swollen vein
in an unguarded moment, a brown
stain was deftly stapled. it is as if great
and dull boulders fill her from the

inside and she withholds her from
herself as if from a grater. *this* she knows:
nobody will ever again breathlessly
peel desire from her shoulders.

when tight is loose

it must have happened gradually, but
she feels overcome—suddenly her body
is simply loose, as if nothing wants
to be firmly tied and trim. for example
her teeth, hair, everything down to her
pelvic floor is now loose, even her

eyes bubble—the left one with its own
eccentric jumpiness. here is the upper lip
plying the accordion and yesterday when
she pointed at something, her upper arm
flapped its own new suede purse—
her fingers are crumbling away and refuse

to open bottles, taps or masturbate.
her stomach lies like a dish in her lap.
there are blue medallions on her thighs
and if she *has* to look down, she sees
her knees shrinking like forgotten
prunes in a bowl. her skin is loose from

her flesh like a shuddered boiled-milk
skin. what should be tight, is loose
and what should be loose is very
tight, because if she looks left all
her shoulders simply have to turn as well;
it is last year she saw her haunches last

in the *Hormone Book* by Susan Mare
she reads about the wane
of oestrogen: the waist thickens and
the vagina wall thins and the colon crashes
through its own arse. how dare her toe
nails grow so riotous then, thicken so

yellowish while she is loosening at the
seams and simply falling away? since
when has her blood impulse changed
from 'fuck off' to 'careful now'?
since when have her transgressions
fallen back to half a marijuana zol since

when has her memory gone more than
it comes? since when has she been aware that
the brain is looking for bridges across
the dying of nerve ends at the outer
edges of the skin? since when have the tiny
sprouts in the ear been calcifying and

the retina lost its ability to delight
in bright colours? when did the brain
let go of the slaked tongue? why does
the nose yearning for youth have
to muffle forth with an expired prostate?
mornings her piss smells like wet cement

softsift of the hourglass

half of her is somebody else
as if   somebody else
is standing next to her *in* her like
the bridge of a nose   her brain
tolls and tolls and keeps on tolling
    she opens the shower   her left
    cheek soaks in the spray until warm
    inside   her right
cheek hangs   cold and dull on
the outside   her blood pressure
rears and rears and keeps on rearing
a chipped shoulder knob   the other
glad and gleaming   the breasts hang
wide-eyed in front of a heart which bangs blood
deafening through all the veins
her body resounds from her lymph
the left hand   has lost its grip
it fumbles like a dishcloth at the soap
the right does not know   what the left is doing
only one hand   washes the lame
the left as egg whisk   pale stalled fountain
disintegrating mop   wilting lily
blood begins to crawl   where once it
    ran
but it is the left leg
that she misses most
the light-footed turn   the swank of swerve
the quick sidestep in jest—
enraged she rips into everything
inside herself, but quivering in her ribs
one can see that already
she's been by the half-dead dead eclipsed

some seasonal observations of Table Mountain

WINTER
wednesday 18 june
I cannot look at you
today, not today. with eyes averted
from your stony perfection
I do my daily chores.

over my terrified
body my hand moves up to
my breast again hoping
that the lump of clay will not be there
that the hand misconstrued

the mountain stands
stripped clean and burnt through. I live by the
breath of this mountain alone.
I have no other competence. on
the windward side fringes of light sing, on
the lee side there is nought

not even a single
line that knows of me. mortality
sticks to my lip like sweat.
I want to know/not to know/to know
everything/know nothing

thursday 19 june
invisible mountain this morning
in this mist—a lump of grief against
which everything flounders.
softly your thoughts try to probe around
it   gently you sense the
embedded stone, the numbness of it

the immobility,
you don't have the courage to fathom
the full extent, you just
await the result. from the waist up you
blindly suppose yourself
secretly whole, you try to defuse

your body's insurgence
against your body. let the stone lump
grow cold in the fog, let
the pine trees tilt like umbrellas in
a cortège, let my thoughts
steam to ripeness in sorrow. but I,

I am occupied this
morning: softly I coax my breasts to
unwind in foam, let them
freely drowse in tranquil fragrance
rinse them in honey
to luminous shape and there where
the mammogram reveals its
blackest clot, I lather in light
and
light-
limbed
bliss
so

blindingly that the black membrane
feels
itself blessed, diluting its
toxic polyps,
dissolving them to effluence. see
the rust bleeding away like biestings.

whole like a whiplash

I *want* to live on this earth.
                    (late night)
fuck-all. I feel fuck-all
for the life hereafter—it's *now* that
I want to live, *here*

is what I want

sunday 22 june
nothing arrives. my throat
constricts. a resigned grief burns up in
my chest, smoking. my heart
whimpers on her hinges. I want to
touch something, hold something,
revive the wholeness that once was mine.

I want to return with
my previous body. I am not
I, without my body
only through my body can I in-
habit this earth. my soul
is my body entire. my body

embodies do not
turn against me, oh do not
ever leave me. do not
cave in around me, do not plummet
away from me, do not
die off on me, step
into the breach for me—
my only mandate to
engage the earth

friday 27 june
the last rains of winter fall
faster than the yearning of winter trees
with lymphatic systems
against the wintry light. benign
benign it sings—it's as if
I am young again in
my upper arms, suddenly, and smooth

at the back of my head.
my body glows complete, my elbows
hang free with my senses
extended over my skin.
I want to
ascend
in *this* body
roaring its immaculate radiance

(all poems in this section published in Verweerskrif, *2006)*
(translated by Andries Wessels)

on my behalf

i no longer need to approach anybody on someone's behalf
i no longer need to be accountable for others
or to ask forgiveness on behalf of those who know no guilt

i no longer need to put anybody's marginalised
perspective on the table or imagine
myself into the skin of another

because the first forays of death have arrived
and the body slips like sand through
the fingers   apathy neutralises the senses

as survival deploys its brutal forces   one gets cut
off from others and becomes more and more
familiar with the complete inward-turning of death—

drawer after drawer you are being emptied out
until only your empty inside moves your emptiness about

(Verweerskrif, 2006)

ABOUT THE POET

Antjie Krog has won major awards in almost all the genres and media in which she has worked: poetry, journalism, fiction, and translation. Krog's first volume of poetry was published when she was seventeen years old and she has since released thirteen volumes of poetry, receiving nearly every literary award available in South Africa for works in Afrikaans and English. She is married to architect John Samuel, and is the mother of four children.

TRANSLATORS FROM AFRIKAANS INTO ENGLISH

Karen Press is a South African poet who has published eight collections of poetry.

Denis Hirson is a South African novelist, poet and essayist.

Patrick Cullinan is an award-winning South African poet who has published nine collections of poetry.

Andries Wessels is a professor of English, translator, and author.